GRAND DEPARTURES

Books in the Lowestoft Chronicle Anthology Series

LOWESTOFT CHRONICLE 2011 ANTHOLOGY
FAR-FLUNG AND FOREIGN
INTREPID TRAVELERS
SOMEWHERE, SOMETIME...
OTHER PLACES
GRAND DEPARTURES

"Full of great talent and exceptionally well written pieces. An entertaining read."   —Tara Smith, *The Review Review* (5-Star Review)

"*Lowestoft Chronicle* is a wonderful new addition to the world of creative writing."   —Tony Perrottet, acclaimed author of *The Naked Olympics*

"The *Lowestoft Chronicle* is unique. Of course there's the humor, which has heft even when it's laugh-out-loud funny. But even more than I enjoy the humor, I appreciate the serious skill with which the authors have practiced their craft and value the surprising imaginative stance of this or that storyteller, poet, or essayist to his or her far-flung subject and the put-you-there vividness of the rendering."   —David Havird, poet, author of *Map Home*

"*Lowestoft Chronicle* is a standout among a growing universe of online journals. Every issue delivers a cornucopia of entertaining and thought-provoking stories and articles."   —Michael C. Keith, acclaimed author of
The Next Better Place: A Father and Son on the Road

"A brilliant, savory, sharp, amusing and varied taste of my favorite magazine, *Lowestoft Chronicle*. I'm delighted that a place exists for this kind of travel writing. Nicholas Litchfield has put together something very special, something to celebrate, enjoy, savor."
                    —Jay Parini, internationally bestselling author of
The Last Station and *The Passages of H.M.*

"The *Lowestoft Chronicle* is both classy and fun to read. A work accomplished by careful attention to detail and quality."
                    —Sheldon Russell, award-winning author of
Dreams to Dust and the Hook Runyon mystery series

"Terrific anthology. The writing here is fresh, surprising, and alive. The book looks and feels great. If you aren't familiar with *Lowestoft Chronicle*, head on over there. They publish, on a consistent basis, excellent fiction, poetry, and non-fiction."   —Nicholas Rombes, acclaimed author of
A Cultural Dictionary of Punk: 1974-1982

"*Lowestoft Chronicle* is a superb lit mag. It offers the kind of perceptive, humorous writing that we like here at TCR." —*The Committee Room*

"A fun read." —*New York Journal of Books*

"How did I not know about the *Lowestoft Chronicle*? If you're late to this travel and literary parade as well, check out Nicholas Litchfield's superb online journal specializing in all things to do with travel, literature, and the overlap between these life-nourishing activities."

— James R. Benn, acclaimed author of the Billy Boyle World War II mystery series

"The much-admired *Lowestoft Chronicle*, an eclectic and innovative online journal…[offers] a mouth-watering feast of short stories, poems, narrative non-fiction, and in-depth interviews with acclaimed authors. This vibrant literary forum is the brainchild of author and editor Nicholas Litchfield, an English-born librarian who lives in Western New York. Packed into the pages are stories to entice, enthral, and entertain… incisive and enlightening interviews…[and] a tasty blend of pleasing and deftly prepared poems." —*Lancashire Evening Post*

"The literary equivalent of Rick's Café in *Casablanca*, where travelers of all stripes pull up a stool and swap stories at the bar. Handsomely designed and expertly curated, *Lowestoft Chronicle* drives us into the arms of experience." —Scott Dominic Carpenter, acclaimed author of *Theory of Remainders*

"I'm always impressed with the quarterly online literary magazine, *Lowestoft Chronicle*—it's filled with intriguing fiction, non-fiction, poetry, and interviews. Click on over for good reading."

—Matthew P. Mayo, Spur Award-winning author of *Tucker's Reckoning*

"*Lowestoft Chronicle*'s website is nicely laid out and there is wide variation of reading material." —Henry F. Tonn, Newpages.com

"*Lowestoft Chronicle* publishes some of the finest work of travel writing on the Internet today. I was enthralled by the work, by the control in narrative each of the contributors have. Like a new lover, *Lowestoft Chronicle* fascinated me more times over than I anticipated, and I believe that it is something the journal aims for and will continue to do."

—Krystal Sierra, *The Review Review* (5-Star Review)

"Reading *Lowestoft Chronicle* is like jostling through a sprawling bazaar in Tashkent or Ulaanbaatar, with eyes wide open and wits on high alert. Invigorating, too." —Victor Robert Lee, author of *Performance Anomalies*

"I was extremely impressed with the variety and quality of the writing. There's something here for everyone. A solid collection of funny and fine travel-themed stories, poetry, essays and interviews that easily fits in a back pocket or carry-on bag." — Frank Mundo, Examiner.com

"Nicholas Litchfield's selection of stories, poems, memoirs and interviews is a treasure for readers who enjoy a good dose of humor with their armchair travel." —Mary Donaldson-Evans, author of *Madame Bovary at the Movies* and *Medical Examinations*

"This is the only literary magazine I read these days, and it's always enjoyable. It takes the reader to a wide variety of literary destinations, and makes even a confirmed hermit like me want to get up and go somewhere. Highly recommended." —James Reasoner, *New York Times* bestselling author

"The concept and the layout are wonderful...WOW."
—Abby Frucht, author of the *New York Times* Notable Books *Life Before Death*, *Snap*, and *Are You Mine?*

"*Lowestoft Chronicle* is contemporary and worldly but with a sepia charm. It's a Baedeker for the vicarious traveler in the age of globalization."
—Ivy Goodman, award-winning author of *Heart Failure* and *A Chapter from Her Upbringing*

GRAND DEPARTURES

EDITED BY NICHOLAS LITCHFIELD

FOREWORD BY ROBERT GARNER McBREARTY

Lowestoft
Chronicle
Press

GRAND DEPARTURES

SUBMISSIONS

The editors welcome submissions of poetry and prose. For submission information please visit our website at www.lowestoftchronicle.com or email: submissions@lowestoftchronicle.com

Published by Lowestoft Chronicle Press, Cambridge, Massachusetts
www.lowestoftchronicle.com

First edition: November 2016

Cover and book design by Tara Litchfield

ISBN 13: 978-0-9825365-8-2
ISBN 10: 0-9825365-8-5

Library of Congress Control Number: 2016910442

Printed in the United States of America

CONTENTS

FICTION

POETRY

INTERVIEW

CREATIVE NON-FICTION

FOREWORD

Robert Garner McBrearty

I've been reading literary magazines, and publishing in them, for over thirty years, but it is always a pleasure to make a new discovery. I can't quite recall why I sent my story "After Zombies" to *Lowestoft Chronicle*. There was something appealing about the description of the magazine, wherever it was that I came across it. The magazine was interested in travel, I gathered, and in humor, but not exclusively. In fact, there was something rather open and charming about the description. The description somehow made me think of a kindly voice saying, "Come in, come in," as if there were a great desire to make one's acquaintance. The magazine just sounded, well, fun. Lively, eclectic, not quite traditional. Images came to mind: Travelers telling tales in English pubs, windswept seashores, old libraries, a cottage in the woods—oh, and of course, the cottage had to have a fireplace and it had to have someone (me?) sitting in a cozy chair reading. But then, perhaps, the cozy chair is upended and the reader, moments ago comfy in the chair, finds himself transported to a fast-moving train, standing between the cars, wind in his hair, headed to—who-knows-where.

I sent a note along with the story saying that the story was only about "travel" in a broad sense—perhaps the travel of the imagination—but that it did, I hoped, contain some humor. To my pleasure, the story was accepted, and as well, Nicholas Litchfield asked if I'd be interested in an interview. I was. What followed was a series of delightful, thorough exchanges. I mention this not to call attention so much to my own interview as to say what a tremendous interviewer Nicholas is, and I trust readers will discover in all the issues of the magazine similar, fine, in-depth interviews.

Lowestoft Chronicle is not quite like any literary magazine I'm familiar with. It is fun, edgy at times, international in its scope. It surprises. The work is a blend of the serious and the comical, dark shades, light shades, and as I said, ever surprising. Characters and situations change dramatically in the scope of a few pages, as in "A Normal Country" by Ryan Napier. I won't give too much away here, but I think one might say there is no quite normal country in *Lowestoft Chronicle*. And that is a good thing. In reading this fine journal, one discovers the world afresh. And one feels fortunate to hear that voice, kindly inviting, "Come in, come in."

INTRODUCTION

Nicholas Litchfield

"A brilliant, savory, sharp, amusing and varied taste of my favorite magazine, *Lowestoft Chronicle*. I'm delighted that a place exists for this kind of travel writing—if that's a term for it. This is just great writing about place, ranging from the spirit of place to the human spirit. Take it with you on your next trip, no matter how far or flung."

> — Jay Parini, internationally bestselling author of
> *The Last Station* and *The Passages of H.M.*

It has been seven years since *Lowestoft Chronicle* (the first and only literary magazine to come out of the coastal town of Lowestoft, in Suffolk, England) opened its doors to submissions. In that time, we've published more than two dozen issues and six anthologies—*Grand Departures* included. Over the years, the magazine has been described as many things—thankfully, the comments have been positive. Reporter and author Victor Robert Lee's assessment remains one of my favorites: "Reading *Lowestoft Chronicle* is like jostling through a sprawling bazaar in Tashkent or Ulaanbaatar, with eyes wide open and wits on high alert. Invigorating, too." And while the general theme is travel, the broad subject area is such that it allows for a rewarding diversity of content, underscored by Mary Beth Magee, reviewer for Examiner.com, who observed, "The stories and poems vary in tone from dead serious to delightful whimsy, offering something for every taste. Humor, adventure and mystery share the pages with intriguing result."

The submissions we get have always been extremely varied, but I think, generally speaking, the magazine appeals to the more inquisitive, adventurous type of writer wanting (in Magee's words) to "bring the far corners of the world to the reader's armchair." Being open to a wide variety of genres—everything from horror, science fiction and fantasy, to crime, mystery, and westerns (all of which we've published)—is also an advantage. Essentially, the chief obstacle to publication in just about any reputable magazine has everything to do with the quality of the writing.

Some years ago, the literary review website NewPages.com remarked of *Lowestoft Chronicle*, "many of the works take one to places faraway and exotic." It's fair to say that this continues to be the case, but also worth noting that the reader is not necessarily transported to the sort of exquisitely grand destinations that the mind may at first conjure up. Here, the more far-flung stories include Bill Cole's insightful "Unsquared," where a small, technologically disadvantaged community in a remote village in Upper Egypt endeavors to remain unaffected by the escalating social unrest in the region. In "Bago Station," by Elaine Barnard, an industrious local guide in Bago, Myanmar, goes Buddhist-shrine-hopping as she escorts two feeble sightseers across the bustling city. And in Namrata Poddar's "Ladies Special," those aboard the rowdy, overcrowded express train through Mumbai find ways to cope (and multi-task) during the long, taxing commute from work.

Elsewhere, in Paris, a student tries to elude uniformed bus and rail security agents as she attempts to ride the city for free in Justine Dymond's "Metro," while in "Real Mickey" by Nancy Scott Hanway, a toddler's holiday at Disneyland develops into a relentless hunt for Mickey Mouse's home.

Sometimes austere or unpleasant or horrendous, sometimes confusing or disconcerting or perilous—real or imaginary—you're never sure where you'll wind up. In sharp, sardonic stories like "A Normal Country," by Ryan Napier, an obstinate father in Narodistan travels to Florida on a dogged quest to rescue his daughter and bring her home safely. In William Quincy Belle's topical tale of apt retribution, "The Trojan Horse," Russian computer hackers experience a hostile disruption to their activities when one of their victims drops by for a little chat. And Olga Wojtas offers up a dangerous, atypical scenario in her droll story "Crystal Clear," concerning a married couple who quickly regret winning a luxury holiday for two when they're caught in the middle of a foreign revolution.

Several stories serve to remind us of the dangers of the great outdoors. In "Everything That Lives," by Jim Plath, disaster awaits two youths on an innocuous weekend ramble in the woods; in "River High," by Michael C. Keith, a trio of carefree campers put their boating skills to the test when they embark on a hazardous canoe trip across the Gasconade River in south-central Missouri; and early into their six-month road trip across the western U.S., a couple's new relationship is tested when they're caught in a heavy storm in South Dakota's Badlands, in Christina Selby's "Deeper In."

As with previous anthologies, you'll also find here a fine array of fiction and nonfiction to tickle the funny bone, such as Robert Mangeot's "What Settles After the Stars," in which an outspoken wine critic in France seeks absolution for his entertainingly scathing reviews. In Tina Koenig's "Michelangelo Doesn't Cut It," the narrator finds herself in Florence, Italy, contemplating Michelangelo's sculpture of David from a distinctly Jewish perspective. And in Scott Solomon's outrageously funny "Second Opinion," a stunted teenage boy suffers the humiliation of an extensive full-body examination by his mother and pediatrician as they scrutinize his various organs and confer over his physical development.

In other pieces, communities come together and friendships are forged. Near an army base in southern New Mexico, the soft sounds of crackling flames and hypnotic chanting give way to pounding drums and gunfire, as tourists and Native Americans enjoy festivities in Caroline Horwitz's "Pueblo Christmas." In the spirit of liberty, a group of American graduate students celebrate the Fourth of July in a Moroccan themed restaurant in the heart of Prague, Czech Republic, in "Independence Day," by Eileen Cunniffe. In "Festa," by Roland Barnes, Minhoto folk music and makeshift fireworks draw an English couple staying in Portugal out of their remote, ramshackle farmhouse and into a full-blown festival. And in "Swing Low, Sweet Chariot," by Nancy Ford Dugan, a familial unity develops between a group of cab drivers and their regular fare.

And then, of course, there's the flip side to travel— sometimes, your travel companion can turn out to be such a pain in the rear that you wish you'd never taken them up on their offer of a free ride. Case in point: Liz Dolan's witty "Road Kill," where a woman's trip to Martha's Vineyard becomes an exasperating quest to be rid of her insufferable acquaintance.

Poetry has been a staple part of the magazine since we launched our first issue more than six years ago. We've tried to maintain a high standard, yet keep the selections distinctive and varied. I like to think that of the ones included here, like the wickedly comic exploratory poem "Inside the Great Bartender," by Colin Dodds (of whom the late, great Norman Mailer described as showing "something that very few writers have; a species of inner talent that owes very little to other people"), there is much to admire and enjoy. Actually, Dodds provided this much more eloquent description of his work: "A poem from the vanished golden age of not giving a damn, courtesy of the classy cognoscenti at the *Lowestoft Chronicle*."

Doug Bolling and J.E.A. Wallace also conjure up unique perspectives, this time drawing inspiration from travel. In "Out There," Bolling, with his intriguing mustachioed passenger in the smoking jacket and Argyle socks, reminds us of the wonders of travel and that just as every journey yields a story, on every airplane there's a cabin full of travelers with a tale to tell. In "A Year's Worth Of Postcards From London," Wallace offers snapshots of the seasons as he peers with fascination at the changing landscapes out the train window.

Other poems include David Havird's "Downhill from the Marble Village," in which he bemoans the unhappy consequences of inappropriate footwear for a demanding hike; Gina Ferrara's vividly descriptive "Ode to the Indigenous"; Frank Mundo's figurative "re: Your Brother"—drawing from personal tragedy, the poet reflects on his final image of his late sibling—and "Artemis," Ashley Mace Havird's tongue-in-cheek exploration of the island of Sifnos in Greece and its religious relics.

Of all the author interviews published in the magazine, the one included here with short story maestro Robert Garner McBrearty (a recipient of numerous writing awards, including a Pushcart Prize) is our most ambitious yet. Lengthier than normal, it is also the most comprehensive interview McBrearty has given to date. Though primarily focused on his extraordinary debut novel, *The Western Lonesome Society*, other topics discussed include his experiences as a student at the prestigious Iowa Writers' Workshop, as well as in-depth explorations of many of his stories and characters. The anthology also contains his wonderful flash fiction piece "After Zombies," a wildly comic telephone exchange between author and agent as they desperately try to brainstorm a winning idea for a story. (Surely I can't be the only one who thinks that each of the author's absurdly whacky story ideas would make for fantastic reading!)

As with "After Zombies," none of the fine writers in this collection are short on ideas. Dark or comic, poignant or inspiring, thrilling or intricate, there's something for every palate. In the words of Jay Parini, the great and beloved poet, biographer, and storyteller, "Go anywhere with *Lowestoft*. And enjoy the trip." Safe travels!

A NORMAL COUNTRY

Ryan Napier

My daughter's feet were very white.

I saw this, one day, suddenly. It was April. The snow was melting. I climbed the stairs to our apartment. I was cold and sweaty, and my boots were covered in mud.

I opened the door, and she was there.

She was three years old. She had kicked off her house shoes. Her feet were bare and white and very small, and she was there, waiting for me.

I cried.

My daughter told me to stop. My wife came into the hall and asked what had happened. I could not explain.

Every man thinks that his daughter is the finest, the purest, and the most beautiful of all girls. But in my case, it was true: my daughter was truly the finest, the purest, and the most beautiful girl in Narodistan.

———— ✦ ————

She was born in the Communist years.

I had never been political. When I was a boy, I hurt my ankle at Young Pioneer camp, and I never earned a single badge. I didn't care about communism or capitalism. I wanted a wife and a job and friends—a good, normal life.

But then I had my daughter. I changed. I began to *see* and to *think*.

I saw that our cars were from Romania, and our chairs were from Moldova, and none of them worked. I thought of *her*, being taken away from me to sing with the Young Pioneers. I saw the people that drank, during the day, in the playgrounds behind their apartment blocks. I thought of her white feet stuffed into a pair of holey Belarusian boots. I saw that we were a shabby country—all concrete and statues. I thought of Canada and Sweden and Denmark—places where people were clean, and safe, and had good jobs.

I still didn't care about communism or capitalism. I only wanted to give those white feet a clean road through life.

When she was four, the protests started. I joined them. I marched and sang and shouted. The others carried signs and slogans; I held up her picture.

I wanted to give her a normal country—and I did. Narodistan left the Soviet Union. The concrete got clean. The drunks left the playgrounds. We found good jobs and bought computers. Our cars were from Japan, and our chairs were from Sweden.

My daughter did not remember Communism. She did not remember the protests. She went to high school and learned from the new textbooks. She studied English. She was accepted at the University of Narodistan, and we were all very happy.

She wore Italian boots. The revolution worked.

—————— ✦ ——————

She finished high school in May. She would start at the university in September. She wanted to travel.

I was proud. When I was young, foreign travel was banned. But now my daughter was going to be a woman of the world.

I asked where she wanted to go. Sweden? Canada? Denmark?

She showed me a website. U.S. Department of State, it said. Special program for citizens of all former Soviet republics. Summer working holiday visas—hundreds of jobs available. Practice English, earn money, and see America.

She had studied the list of jobs. She wanted to be a lifeguard. She wanted to go to Florida.

I was scared to send her to America. I read the news. I knew that bad things happened in America. Americans were always getting shot—in schools, in malls, on the streets, in their homes. And if they weren't getting shot, then they were protesting: protesting about getting shot, or not having enough guns, or having the wrong president. America looked like Narodistan before the revolution.

I tried to keep an open mind. Maybe it was a normal country after all. Maybe she would be safe.

And then I read about Florida.

I read about storms and floods, drugs and guns, swamps and death. I read about fear and heat and madness. I read about men who used reptiles as weapons.

In Florida, men killed women, and women killed women. Parents killed children, and children killed parents. More people died in shopping malls in Florida than in any other place on earth. Florida had something called a "sinkhole"—a big hole in the ground that could open without warning and swallow a man or a house.

Her white feet would sink down into the swamp.

———— ✦ ————

I told my daughter that she couldn't go. For three days she didn't speak to me.

"What's wrong with Canada?" I said. "Canada has beaches."

My daughter laughed.

"I love you," I said. "I don't want you to die in a shopping mall."

She locked herself in her room.

My wife wanted to let her go. "Of course the U.S. isn't safe," she said. "That's why she wants to go. She's a kid. Kids want to have adventures."

"Fine," I said. "Let her have adventures. Let her have *normal* adventures. When I was her age, I wanted to go to

21

Turkey and wear a robe and ride a horse across the sand. Let her go to Turkey, to Italy, to Russia even—somewhere safe! Some place where the ground won't swallow her up. She can have adventures without dying."

My wife did not agree. She paid the money, and the Americans sent my daughter a visa.

I worried. I stayed up late and read articles on the Internet. American food was full of chemicals—what would my daughter eat? And Americans hated labor—what if they tried to cheat her? Was there a lifeguards' union to help her? And those American police—who would protect her from *them*?

I scrolled and scrolled. There were whole websites about the things that happened in Florida.

We needed a code word, I decided. We needed a special phrase. If my daughter were in trouble—kidnapped, enslaved, trapped in a shopping mall—she could call us and say the word, and I would help.

I suggested some words. But my wife and daughter would not listen. We don't need a word, they said. It's just America.

She bought a one-way ticket. "Don't get a return trip," I said. "You may want to come home sooner." I gave her ten thousand roubles.

My wife said it was too much. "She can fly to Narodistan five times for that."

It didn't matter. She could spend it all if it brought her back one day sooner.

———— ✦ ————

Every Sunday, my wife and I woke at 5:00 a.m. We opened our laptop, and there was our daughter's face—beaming across the Internet, from Florida to Narodistan. It was still evening there. We wore our pajamas, and she wore hers. We talked for an hour, and then she went to sleep. For the rest of the morning, I was happy. I knew she was sleeping. For a few hours, she was safe.

Her face looked a little different. A little changed. I tried not to notice.

She saw many things. She went to Disney World. She shot fireworks. She ate a pie made of limes. I asked if she had seen any guns. She had. I asked her to come home.

The summer passed. She saved a man from drowning.

Finally, it was August. Her visa expired at the end of the month. "When is your flight?" I asked.

She said she needed money. "What about the ten thousand roubles?" I said. "What about your *work*? Are they not paying you? Have you taken this up with the lifeguards' union?"

She apologized. They did pay her. But Disney World, fireworks, pies made of limes—these things were expensive.

I wired her another ten thousand roubles. I waited. The next Sunday, we opened our computer. Her face was not there. We waited. An hour passed. My wife made tea and ate an orange. I hated her for it. I hated her for eating when our daughter was missing.

I called the police. They said they could not solve crimes in the United States. I read things on the Internet. I called the Narodi embassy in Washington, and I left them many messages.

At six o'clock, my daughter's face appeared. I did not hide my tears. "When is your flight?" I said.

She did not have a flight. She was not coming home. She had met a man—a Florida man. She was in love.

———— ✦ ————

She and the Florida man had used my twenty thousand roubles. They had bought a little house. She told us the address and asked us to send some of her things. She said that we could keep her winter clothes. She wouldn't need them in Florida.

I stared at her image on the screen. There she was. It looked like her, alone, in a room. But was there someone else? Was *he* there? Was the Florida man standing just beyond the frame, holding his gun, forcing her to say these terrible things?

We should have had a code word.

She hung up. I called Interpol. I left more messages for the ambassador.

I got ill. I stayed in bed. My wife brought me tea, but I couldn't drink. I was in too much pain.

Until now, I had never felt real pain. I had seen other people in pain. I had heard them moan, and I had wondered why they did it. *Stay silent*, I had thought, *save your energy*. But now I understood moaning. A moaner has no choice. He *must* moan.

I had a steam jet of pain in me. I had to release it. I moaned and moaned.

I tried to sleep. I may have dreamed.

In my half-sleep, I remembered a movie I had seen. An American movie. I could not stop thinking about it. In the movie, there is an American man. His daughter goes to Europe. She is captured by evil men. So this American man goes to Europe. He brings so many guns. He searches for his daughter, and he kills and kills and kills. And then he finds her.

This man is crazy, of course. In this situation, a man from a normal country would call the police. Only an American would solve a problem with so many guns and so much death.

And this was the kind of man who had taken my daughter— an American! What could the ambassador and Interpol do against a man like that?

It all made sense. It was a terrible truth. If I wanted to save her from an American, I had to become an American.

———— ✦ ————

The next morning, I waited outside the U.S. embassy. I told them I needed a visa as soon as possible. I paid a lot of money, and I got it.

My wife wanted to come. "I want to see her," she said. "I

24

want to bring her things."

I was not bringing anything, I said. I was bringing her home.

"Maybe she really is in love," said my wife. "Maybe she's happy."

"Who could be happy in a swamp?"

I flew to the swamp. I landed in Miami. There were thousands of legs and feet. They wore shorts and plastic sandals. They were round and tan. I got sick of legs and feet.

I rented a car. It had strange numbers—miles instead of kilometers. I never knew how fast I was going.

I drove to my daughter's address. It was in a town called Leisure City. The town was on the edge of the Everglades—the big swamp. I had read about it on the Internet. Last year, a man in Leisure City had been arrested for biting a parrot.

I came to the address. Shangri-La Mobile Home Park, it said. The houses were not houses at all. They looked like train cars.

I knocked. My daughter answered. I moaned.

She wore shorts, a shirt, and plastic sandals. She had been eating the chemical food, and she had grown a little stout. She was tan. Her feet were not beautiful.

I told her to get in the car. She shut the door. I heard English from inside. The Florida man appeared. He was stout too, and short. He had hair on his chin, and his shirt had no sleeves. He held out his hand. I did not shake it.

He smiled a lot. He gestured for me to come in, to sit down. They had a couch and two chairs. I stood.

He spoke to me, and my daughter translated. He said he was glad to meet me, that he loved my daughter. He was happy that I had supported them when they wanted to buy a house. He said he would work hard and pay me back.

I told my daughter to get in the car. She shook her head. "Why?" I asked. "Is it unsafe? Is he keeping you? Does he have a gun?"

She translated, and the Florida man smiled. He opened a drawer. He took out a gun.

"I will return!" I shouted this from my car, and I hoped that she heard.

I drove to the police. In my bad English, I explained. The man had a gun. The police did not understand. They asked: "What was his crime?"

"Gun," I said. "Gun, gun, gun."

"A gun isn't a crime," they said.

I thought I understood. I thought they were like the old Soviet police—back when our country was like this. I tried to give them some money. "And now it is a crime?" I said.

They told me to leave.

I drove to a hamburger restaurant. I ate a hamburger, and I thought. I remembered that American action movie. I remembered that American father, with all his weapons and his muscles.

I understood my mistake. I was not yet enough of an American.

——— ✦ ———

I drove around until I saw a Wal-Mart. This, I knew, was a famous American store—famous because it had everything. I went inside. They truly did have everything. They even had guns.

There was a special glass counter full of pistols, and behind it was a big rack of rifles. The man asked me which gun I wanted. "I don't care," I said. He gave me a rifle. "Fine," I said. I gave him my money.

He told me to come back in two days. A waiting period, he explained.

"I need it now," I said.

If I wanted that, he said, I had to go to a gun show. If you bought it at the gun show, you didn't have to wait at all.

So I went. The gun show was at a basketball arena. On the court, there were hundreds and hundreds of tables, and all the tables had guns. I bought a pistol from a big fat man. He was very helpful. He put the bullets in the gun, and he smiled a lot.

It was late. I went to a hotel. I watched cop shows on television, and I noted how they held their guns. I bought potato chips from a machine, ate them on my bed, and fell asleep.

———— ♦ ————

In the morning, I went back to Shangri-La.

My daughter answered the door. "Where is he?" I asked.

"A job interview," she said. "He's going to drive an airboat."

I did not know what an airboat was and I did not want to know. I told her to get in the car.

She said no. I told her that I had a gun now. "I can protect you," I said. She laughed. I showed her the gun, and she laughed some more. She kissed me on the head, said that she loved me, and told me to go home.

I could not understand. Here she was, stout and tan, living in a train car with this little man and his gun. I was going to save her, to bring her back to the normal country that I had worked so hard to give her. There was nothing to stop us now, and yet she would not leave.

"I don't want to leave," she said. "I'm happy." But she could not be happy. Not like this. The Florida man had done something to her mind. But what?

I thought. I remembered what I had read on the Internet.

I kissed her. "I will return," I said.

I drove back to the police. They remembered me and told me to leave. "Listen," I said, "my daughter has been drugged!"

The police got very excited. They started their cars and turned on their sirens. I followed them to Shangri-La.

The Florida man was back. He held my daughter close. The police went into the train car. They opened the cabinets and drawers. They ripped up the carpet. They searched his car. But they could not find his drugs.

"He must have put them all into her," I said.

The police checked our documents. They asked my daughter for her green card. She showed them her visa. It was expired. They started talking about deportation.

"I am her father," I said. "I will take her home."

The police said they would come back in twenty-four hours and if they found my daughter, they would give her to Homeland Security.

She was saved. The Florida man cried and for the first time in months, I was happy. I felt like I had beaten the Russians all over again. The Florida man tried to speak to me, but I told my daughter not to translate. There was no need for English now. Adventures were over. I would put the gun in the trash. We would fly back to Narodistan. Her classes would begin. The stoutness would melt away and the tan would fade.

INDEPENDENCE DAY

Eileen Cunniffe

I leaned back into deep, silky cushions, still savoring the tang of mint and cilantro on my tongue. The soup was beginning to warm me from the inside out, taking away the chill of a drizzly afternoon. The sign over the archway that led into this nearly deserted courtyard in an otherwise bustling quarter of the city read *Casablanca*. In our quest for a memorable meal on the last day of our journey, we'd opted for one of the outdoor, bead-curtained canopies with low, plush sofas, even though we would have been much warmer at an inside table—and it would have been far easier to reach the table and the soup, too. Each time a fez-topped waiter entered our little tent, the beads swayed and clacked and a fresh wave of pungent aromas wafted toward us. It never seemed to be the same waiter twice; we wondered if they were taking turns because they had no other customers.

The food—which, except for the soup, we'd eaten with our fingers—and the trance-inducing music being broadcast throughout the neighborhood, made the illusion almost complete. We had, in fact, followed the music through a tangle of cobbled streets to find our Casablanca. Never mind that my three new friends and I were washing down our Moroccan feast (if "cattle salad"—strips of grilled steak over couscous and greens—is in fact a Moroccan dish, and not just a bad translation) with American beer, in honor of the date, July 4th. It's not like we were in Morocco. No, we were in the heart of Prague, in the Czech Republic, where we could just as easily have celebrated Independence Day in TGI Friday's or Pizza

Hut, then popped into a Dunkin' Donuts for dessert.

But for our penultimate meal, just a few hours ahead of a more traditional Czech dinner with a set menu featuring venison, we'd decided to add one last layer of cross-cultural experimentation to our collective memories of Prague. What was a Moroccan restaurant doing in the middle of Prague anyway? Was it an homage to the fictional Czech hero Victor Laszlo? Or had the Moroccans invaded Prague along with America and most of Europe once the free-market economy had begun to take root? And was this culinary discovery any stranger than the disco party on an after-dinner cruise down the Vltava River that we'd experienced the night before or the surreal black-light marionette interpretation of *Yellow Submarine*—dialogue in Czech, soundtrack in English—we'd stumbled upon earlier in the week?

As part of a group of mid-career American graduate students from the University of Pennsylvania who, for a week, had been exploring this beautiful, sometimes eccentric, maze of a city and its surrounding countryside, my friends and I had been embarrassed by the ubiquitousness of American "culture" in Bohemia. It seemed to clash horribly with the elegant profile of the castle that towered above the city, reminding us of Prague's rich and noble history. It was beyond ironic that every tourist map was dotted with golden arches while the words "site of former statue of Stalin" still haunted one high hill nearly 40 years after the statue itself had been toppled.

Yet the dozens of businesspeople, academics, and government workers who had met with our seminar class all week could hardly contain their enthusiasm over the transformations that were taking place across Eastern Europe as foreign businesses moved in, opened shop, and infused much-needed funds and jobs into a newly capitalistic society. Prague was the pulsing heart of a country very much in the midst of self-discovery, mostly driven by the passions of people still in their 20s and

30s. People older than that had generally taken a step or two back; they were happy to participate, but not at all certain of how to lead the charge in a world they no longer recognized.

While we waited for coffee, Maureen, Joe, Dan, and I compared the treasures we'd purchased that morning as we'd poked through a Saturday street market, made one last sweep through the shops around Old Town Square, and strolled among the makeshift stalls on the Charles Bridge: garnet jewelry, marionettes, colorful glass goblets, a pastel drawing, and—the largest purchase of all—a small crystal chandelier for Maureen's foyer. We congratulated ourselves on having collected authentic Czech souvenirs, avoiding the high-priced designer shops that had sprung up just off the square—the same shops we could find at home (tomorrow), in Philadelphia, if we were so inclined.

It seemed funny that the four of us—all second-generation Americans who'd grown up within miles of the Liberty Bell and had lived through the summer-long extravaganza that was the U.S. Bicentennial celebration in 1976—had had to travel so far from home to truly experience the Fourth of July, the sense of being there at the beginning of history in a country that was inventing itself while the world watched with interest, lending seemingly boundless moral and financial support.

I'm not sure I ever fully tasted freedom until that rainy Saturday when I toasted my own nation's birthday in a Moroccan restaurant with a glass of *pivo* (the only Czech word I can recall all these years later) in a newborn-ancient land that only recently had escaped from the clutches of communism. It tasted sweet—and a bit exotic, too.

Our coffee cups were drained, our fingers were growing cold, and we had a lot of packing to do before dinner. We flagged the first fez we spotted, and, for one last time, amused ourselves by saying, "Czech, please."

BAGO STATION

Elaine Barnard

There is no place for me but Bago, once one of the most important cities in Burma, now a forgotten stop on Myanmar's line to Mandalay. I wait each day at Bago Station. There are trains arriving from Yangon every morning and early afternoon. Occasionally, tourists ride the open-air train with the workers. It is cheap (only one US dollar), instead of the bus (for two people it is three-hundred kyat), or the taxi (forty to fifty dollars). They arrive full of train dust, determined to view our great Buddhas and holy altars, to inhale the incense, the cumin and coriander, to lose themselves in the rumble of trucks traveling Bago night and day, making sleep almost impossible.

This morning two persons arrived: a man much older than myself (I am thirty, although some say I look thirteen. It is the rice that does it, a single bowl each morning, like the monks in our monastery on the hill), and an old woman. The man, very white and somewhat weak looking, helped the old woman from the train as if she were parchment and could crack if she did not step carefully. The train steps are steep. Sometimes they are missing altogether and the passengers must leap from the train, throwing their baggage before them.

The train from Yangon to Bago was late this morning. Engine trouble, they said. This is not unusual. The train from Yangon is often late. I wait and wait until dark. Sometimes it does not arrive at all and I am left to bicycle home in the blackness. This is treacherous as the roads are rough; pot holes the size of graves waiting to catch you. I have fallen into several of these, bruising arms and legs, wrecking my bike, which, fortunately, my friend Tan could repair. My second wife bathed my bruises while our baby sloshed in the bath water. "Get another job," she scolded. "This one is too dangerous."

"What other job? There is no job but Bago Station." She knows this as well as I. Tourists are our only income unless we become rice farmers, burning the fields before new planting, our faces black with soot. I tried that when I was younger. She did not like that either. The soot was difficult to wash. I remained black until burning season was over.

My two tourists seem confused. Tourists always look confused. There are no signs telling them which way the great Buddhas lie, or the Rough & Ready hotel, or a toilet to relieve themselves.

I approach, smiling my best smile. "Let me help you. I have lived here all my life."

"Where is the ticket window?" the man asks, wiping the dust from his oversized sunglasses. "We need to book a train back to Yangon this evening."

I lead them to the ticket office. It is a cubicle hidden near the back of the train station. The clerk is nowhere in sight. "He must be at lunch. Sit, he will soon be here." But, of course, there is no place to sit, so they stand, leaning against the doorjamb to rest. Finally, he comes, sipping tea from a thermos.

"Passports?" He swallows slowly, seating himself behind his cluttered desk.

My tourist unfolds them from a money belt hidden beneath his shirt. "Train to Yangon tonight?"

"All booked," the clerk answers, rubbing his belly, which overlaps his belt. "There might be a bus."

"Where is the bus depot?" The old lady looks flustered, as if this could not be happening.

"That way." He points outside.

"Do you have a map?"

The clerk smiles, waving his hand and, chattering in

Burmese, addresses the next person in line. My tourists start to walk, probably thinking they can walk everywhere in Bago. They have no idea of the breadth of this city, how the Buddhas are at opposite ends. It would take a week or more to walk to them all.

I take advantage of the situation. "Come. I will guide you to the bus depot."

The bus depot is almost impossible to find, as it is not really a depot but part of a coffee shop. Feng runs it. She has the schedule. She knows when the last bus to Yangon will arrive. "Five p.m.," she says. "Be here. The bus will not wait."

It is now two in the afternoon. My tourists are gray with train dust and tired. "Come, I will show you the Buddhas."

They hesitate. "Can we walk there?"

"It is too far. I have a friend who will take us. Four passenger bus, very comfortable."

"What is the price?" The man fumbles beneath his shirt.

I knew he would ask that. They always do. It is often the first thing from their mouths. They are afraid we will cheat them. But that is not my custom. I want only what is fair. "Twenty-five kyat," I bargain.

"Twenty," he says.

"Twenty-five," I repeat, thinking if I say it often enough he'll give in.

"Twenty two," he answers firmly.

I agree, tired of repeating myself, but also because I notice two other guides waiting to steal my tourists from me.

My friend, Tan, waits with his tuk-tuk parked in back of the coffee shop. "This is Tan. He will drive us to all the Buddhas."

"We must be back by five." The old lady looks a bit jittery.

"You will be. I promise."

I help them into the tuk-tuk. It is not easy, as the steps are loose and the seat boards rickety. The old lady hits her head on the metal rods upholding the cardboard roof.

"I thought you had a van." She rubs the sore spot on her head.

"This is a van," I shout as Tan revs his motorbike.

The tuk-tuk rocks forward, shooting the old woman across the aisle. Her son catches her.

"We could use some seat belts," she mumbles.

"Yes, I have ordered some from Amazon. They will arrive any day now." I laugh, knowing this is impossible. There is no such service in Bago. Very few have computers. I am hoping to buy one secondhand from one of the monks at the monastery on the hill. The monks have all the money, exacting a price for their prayers. I am sending my oldest son to the monastery, as I can no longer afford to send him to school. He will learn to be a monk, to beg for donations, to chant prayers at certain hours, to obey orders. This last will be difficult for him, as he runs from me whenever I catch him stealing mangoes from our neighbor's garden. Our neighbor sells them in town, so it is not right that my son should steal them.

Tan steers through the vendors selling fruit and fish, chicken and beef, all the foodstuffs that I cannot afford. Flies settle on the chicken, making a home on the gizzards. The smell of overripe bananas overcomes the old lady. She presses a tissue to her nose as if to ward off some disease. I love the perfume of overripe fruit. It is a reminder of plenty.

We approach the Shwemawdaw Pagoda. It is often referred to as the Golden God Temple. It is the tallest pagoda in Myanmar. I help my old lady from the tuk-tuk. She stumbles, gawking at the Golden God.

"Steady." I take her elbow.

A government official approaches. "Ten-dollar entrance." He holds up *Lonely Planet* to prove the entrance fee.

My tourists look surprised. Obviously they have never read this travel guide to Southeast Asia.

"Come." Hurriedly, we reboard the tuk-tuk. I take them

to the secondary entrance. "No fee here. Avoid passing the western gate."

The old lady does not wish to take her shoes off. Perhaps her toes are crooked and she does not wish to show them.

"Mom," her son says, "we have to take our shoes off. It is disrespectful not to."

"I'm not taking them off. That's final." She starts to climb aboard the tuk-tuk. Tan rushes to help her. She smiles at him. He holds her hand longer than is necessary. It is Tan's way. He drives quickly to the other pagodas, as time is growing short.

The Shwethalyaung reclining Buddha is my favorite. It is the second largest Buddha in the world. I could lie beside this Buddha all night. Secretly, I have done this, sneaking in after dark, spending the whole night pressed against its feet, kissing them, praying for my first wife's happiness in the next life. Praying the dengue fever did not accompany her into the world she inhabits now. Praying she is relieved from all sickness, her beauty returned to her, the beauty she lost during the long fever. They could not attend to her at the hospital, as I had no kyat to pay for her care. She was placed on a cot in the corridor and left to die.

"It is four p.m. now," I remind Tan. We have seen the Kyaikpun Pagoda as well, and the Maha Kalyani Sima, and the Mahazedi Pagoda, the Shwegugale Pagoda, and, finally, the Snake Pagoda, which my tourists loved because the entrance was free. "A bit like Disneyland," the old lady blurts, her eyes glazed with pagodas.

I have seen this Disneyland on Feng's TV when I wait for the bus to Yangon. It is true that our colors are bright like Mickey Mouse, the Seven Dwarfs, and Alice in her Wonderland. We take great care of our Buddhas, repainting them often, gilding the stupas, making certain the altars are swept clean. If we are careful of our holy sites in this world, we are promised a better life in the next.

Tan starts his motor. It catches, then stops. I help him give the bike a shove. "Get on," I yell. "Once it gets going we can't stop."

But the old lady won't get on. "Get a taxi. I'm not getting on that thing. I value my life."

"You must get on," Tan pleads. "It is the only way. No taxis out here."

"C'mon, Mom," her son urges. "We'll miss the bus."

"I don't want to die in that contraption," she sobs.

Finally, we carry her on, seating her between us, holding her steady as Tan rocks the motorbike, trying to get it started. Ru—n-ru—n-ru—n. He sweats. Crowds gather, some laughing, some trying to help push the tuk-tuk over the ruts.

"They promised us a new road," Tan calls back. "It is late in coming. Maybe never."

We jolt forward and gradually begin to fly over the ruts as the crowd waves us on. Tan hoots as we speed toward the bus stop. Even the old lady has stopped complaining.

"The bus for Yangon left five minutes ago. It wouldn't wait." Feng sloshes some coffee cups in a pail of water. "Take them to the Rough & Ready. Ask for a room in back. The old lady needs some sleep."

DOWNHILL FROM THE MARBLE VILLAGE

David Havird

I went by public bus to the marble village,
Saturday's end of the line.
Square slabs of marble paved the thoroughfare;
steep marble steps climbed to the upper levels.
Marble the archways that gave on a cavernous
maze of mule tracks, marble paved.

A sign near the bus stop directed me to a church.
How long it would take to walk there and back who knew?
The grassy pathway down was sometimes steep,
with jagged rocks, which pointed upward, and thistles,
not to mention the plastic bottles,
cellophane wrappers, wads of white tissue…

My sandals, right for the port, for my loitering there,
were wrong for hiking downhill from the marble escarpment.
Their rubber foot beds gripped the soles of my feet,
gripped them with sweat like glue—
it was, without much shade, a blistering hike—
while step by step inertia tested the bond
and the least misstep ruptured the grip.

Early Byzantine, the church
belonged to the seventh century, maybe the ninth—
left open page-down on my bed, the guidebook knew—
and boasted if not a kissed-bleary icon,

maybe a soot-dimmed fragment of fresco worth
one's straining to see, if luck had the church unlocked.

The way was not for sandals—I turned back—
much less for shoes, or so the bells,
as I translate their summons, tell;
but rather for feet, bones bruised, soles pierced and bleeding,
the pilgrim's bare feet. I should, they're tolling, the bells
of the portside cathedral this Sunday morning at 7—

I should have kicked those goddamned sandals off.
The site attained and myself shed of my lading,
from that deep vein I'd have as good as winged
my way uphill? No, agony
it had to be returning—this I know—
bedazzling though the destination was
and cool because it was marble.

SWING LOW, SWEET CHARIOT
Nancy Ford Dugan

Jim growls, "My divorce is final." No "hello" as I hop into his cab. He has chronic late-night disc jockey voice, even though it's ten o'clock Saturday morning.

I'm not sure whether to say "Congratulations" or "I'm sorry." It's the first full sentence he's said to me in the six years he's been picking me up. Unless you count "Your train's late," which it often is and he often says, as if I have any control over its schedule. But he is one of the few reliable ones, always waiting for me at the train station and right on time in the afternoon, picking me up to catch the train back to the city.

I go with "Are you happy or sad about it? Or both?" I try to sound neutral, yet polite.

"Well, my wife, she was cheating on me," he says as he pulls onto I-84. "I got to work two jobs. So I'm never home. Day or night. Weekends, I do the cabs. She was stepping out on me."

"Oh, I'm sorry." I stare out the window and feel bad for him. Jim never plays the radio, unlike Eddie who blares The Spinners. But if he did, I sense a country-and-western theme coming on.

"So anyways, I caught her in bed with my friend Harry." He laughs.

Dear Lord. This may be way more than I need to hear. I'm ashamed. For everyone. And does this mean I need to over-tip?

"But I guess it's all right. I got the house. She insisted."

"Well, that's good."

"Yep. Except, I never have time to cut the grass."

We ride in silence.

"Now the women are coming out of the woodwork for me!" He's full of pride. He looks like a demented teacher; his wife fooled around on him, but he's feeling fine. I feel truly cheered on his behalf.

"Well, good for you!"

"Yep. I got two women after me. And they're both named Jane."

"Get out!" I'm positively gleeful.

Jim chuckles. "It gets confusing. I'm never sure who's calling. Whoops, I better get that."

He turns on his cell and checks the face. "Yep. Nope. OK." He ends the call. "I have to check the caller ID to figure out which Jane it is."

———— ✦ ————

That afternoon, Mike picks me up, and for once, he's not literally asleep at the wheel when I climb in. He likes to come early and take a nap in the nursing home parking lot. Mike always asks me how I am, in a meaningful way. I appreciate it and always say I'm fine.

Today, Mom's up to waving good-bye from her window and I'm glad it's Mike. He pulls out of the driveway real slow, giving Mom and me plenty of time for leisurely mutual waving, my arm extended out the cab door window.

Mike's respectfully silent for a minute. "So how was your holiday?" I ask, and he describes each dish of his big meal, down to the collard greens and black-eyed peas. He seems surprised I ever had any. He says his girlfriend of twenty years got mad at him for staying up until 4:30 a.m. with his neighbor watching sports tapes. Usually he works as a cabbie till 6:00 p.m., sleeps till 10:30, and then reports to his night counselor job at a home for abused kids. I think how tired he must always be.

"I restrain their demons," he says.

"It's tough to be a kid," I say.

"You said a mouthful," Mike says. He always takes back roads, as if the highway is just not mellow enough for him.

———■ ✦ ■———

Next week, I get Gabriel in the morning. Gabriel rides low, with the seat full out, even though he is not very tall. As a result, my knees in the backseat are near my chin. He drives in a pleasant hurry. I don't understand much of anything he says in his sweet, high-pitched voice, but at certain angles he resembles a maniacal Antonio Banderas, so I don't care. He tends to hog me and tries to beat the other cabbies picking me up (it's a good-size fare). If he's not the one assigned by the dispatcher, this creates awkwardness and a bit of a rumble, like some James Dean scene in Rebel Without a Cause. The drivers start to yell at each other. I stand and wonder what to do and if I'll be late, while the cabbie testosterone airs itself.

If it's Eddie, it can get ugly. He and Gabriel don't get along. Eddie likes Motown and golf and is, like Jim, a growler. He drives a different route each time, which makes me crazy. He's in power, he's in charge, he's the man. But when he's in a rare good mood, he plays me his old jazz tapes, and they almost make me forgive his quirks.

———■ ✦ ■———

I've never met the dispatcher Susie, but I talk to her every week. She's very protective. Her scratchy voice comes over the cab's speakerphone during every ride: "Do you have her?"

"Yeah. I got her," the cabbies say.

The first year, I guess I was thoughtless to suddenly stop calling for cabs when the golf season ended and my brother started giving me rides. When spring came and I called to arrange the cabs again, Susie let me have it. "We were so worried. We figured, you know, your mom." She drifted off. "I'm relieved to hear from you!"

I felt guilty and now call Susie every week to let her know

if I don't need rides or if I do. It's almost too much. I'm just one car-less city woman making a trip up every weekend to see her mom.

In the city, taxi drivers don't form these kinds of attachments. Except once: The first cab I took after 9/11, the driver started crying and had to pull over. It was early morning, the streets still eerily deserted, the sky foggy gray. Then I started crying as he sat in the front seat in his turban saying "I love America." We were both wiped out after that exchange and stared straight ahead through the grimy windshield. After a while, he started up the cab again and took me to work. There was no possible music to distract us along our way.

During that ride, I recognized a brand-new fear and dread to accompany the one I already had about Mom. It settled in, tucked against the family stress and loss; it, too, was here to stay.

But my cabbies rescue me each week, and rain or shine, they carry me home. And for now, at least, I can't get to Mom and back without them. I expect, when the time comes, oh, how I will miss them.

FESTA

Roland Barnes

In 1995, for the first time since buying a ruined farmhouse in the Alto Minho region of Portugal four years earlier, my wife Diane and I had three whole weeks summer holiday, including a memorable weekend. Preparing the Friday evening meal, we could hear hymn singing in the air; thin voices of supplicant women sounding very eerie from inside our remote house in the woods. Outside it was more distinct, but we had no idea where the sound was coming from and by bedtime it had gone. On Saturday morning, music as different as chalk and cheese boomed out across the valley. This was Minhoto folk music, with its assertive lively melodies sung by alternating male and high-pitched female voices sometimes rising to shrieking pitch, followed by a chorus accompanied by an incessant concertina. It's an "in your face" kind of music, but in a valley full of echoes, it was not easy to locate. By the time it went dark, the sound had changed again to Portuguese pop, and there were flashing lights on the other side of the valley. We didn't want to miss this so jumped into the car and drove in the direction of the lights, which naturally got brighter as we approached.

There is something magical about the combination of bright lights and pop music that draws children to fairgrounds and quickens the steps of football fans moving along the dark terraced streets of northern English towns towards floodlit stadiums. Our destination was *a festa popular* just getting underway. The focus of such festivities is always the parish church and this one was raised up from the main road. What had caught our attention was a triangular frame of twinkling white lamps strung over the church porch with fluorescent lighting streaming from the interior through the open door. Climbing up from the road, the church itself was surrounded by a tall granite wall that sparkled in the moonlight. Inside the boundary, on rows of dining chairs, were elderly men in suits and women in dark dresses, listening to the music and attending to their devotions whenever they felt the need. With a big chestnut tree behind and, beyond that a mountain with a full moon sitting on top, it put me in mind of a work of 1830 by the English painter Samuel Palmer called "Coming from Evening Church": moon, sky, mountain, tree, and church so close as to be almost touching; an intimate little world enveloped in darkness.

Entering the Chapel of O Senhor dos Aflitos, we noticed that the effigy of the saint was casually dumped on the chapel floor, as if arm-weary bearers had dropped him at the first opportunity. (Effigies have a hard time in the Minho. José Saramago has a story about a life-size papier-mâché St. George stationed in Braga Cathedral who took pride of place when strapped to a horse during church processions: "As befits one who rides to do battle with dragons from time immemorial." On one outing, the newly shod horse slipped on the tramlines in the city center, unseating the saint who fell heavily in the roadway. In their distress, the devout spectators made so much noise they disturbed a family of rats living in the saint's innards that fled the toppled effigy, scattering amongst the crowd. Shame and indignation followed and St. George was never allowed out again). In the Minho, these little chapels tend to be unadorned and rather somber places for most of the year but spring into life during festivities. Bunches of lilies and irises from the processional float were unceremoniously scattered about the floor.

The pop music was coming from a *banda* on a scaffolding stage. These bands are usually semi-professional musicians on summer tours. A typical lineup consists of a male singer sounding like Ricky Martin, backed by two flimsily-clad young girls and a rhythm section; sometimes the lead singer is female or there are both sexes fronting the band. It is upbeat Portuguese pop mixed with slow tempo romantic ballads, but many of these musicians are versatile and can turn their hand to folk music or Brazilian samba, especially in the bigger festivals in towns and cities. Before buying a house, we explored north Portugal by train, spending a few nights in some of the main towns. In Braganca, we saw a folk troupe performing in a park, followed on stage later the same evening by a Brazilian samba band. There was a stunning looking girl amongst the folk singers and there she was again in a flouncy "Brazilian" dress. It eventually dawned on me that they were the same people.

There had been rockets firing into the sky and exploding like mortar shells on the scrubby hillside opposite since the previous evening—a practice now forbidden because of fire risk—but it was difficult to work out exactly where they were coming from. All was revealed on a walk through the cobbled pathways of the hamlet before joining the *festa*. Huddled together in an alley a little way from the center of activity were a group of middle-aged men setting off the rockets. Suddenly coming across them, their sly looks gave me the impression of a group of schoolboys caught having a smoke behind the bike shed.

Like most of my generation brought up in the north of England, putting rockets into empty bottles—standing on backyard walls, lighting the blue touchpaper, and retiring just like the instructions said—had been child's play, but this was man's work. These guys were holding the rockets in the palms of their hands, putting a lighted cigarette to the fuse and then, with one arm outstretched, waiting until they hissed away. Including the stick, these missiles were more than a yard long with a thick body of explosive. The villagers were obviously enjoying themselves and grinned widely at me as

I stood watching the rockets fly into the air, waiting for the bang a few second later. It's obviously a dangerous way to have fun, illustrated by the number of elderly men in the villages with missing fingers and thumbs, but the ones setting off the fireworks were probably the most responsible adults in their community, operating far away from the excitable crowds with no sign of children or young people around them.

The wooded drinks hut was serving *vinho verde tinto* dispensed from five-liter plastic flagons into cups like shallow soup bowls; in those days, few local people had a taste for the *branco*. It's easy to please the Portuguese by admiring homegrown produce, but there was no need to feign fondness for the light red bubbling into the pots. Diane was not as enthusiastic as it is high on acidity and soon requested the white, which came conventionally in a glass out of a bottle. That rather characterless Portuguese lager was also available, but in those days we stuck strictly to the wine.

Taking up a position on the edge the crowd, surrounding the rough earth quadrangle that served as a dance floor, our foreignness—coloring, clothing and tendency to brisk walking—attracted attention. Most annoying was the continual staring, an intrusiveness we have never gotten used to. (More recently, we met some fraught tourists from the north of England, in the town of Valenca de Minho. With characteristic candor, the first thing they said was: "Aren't these people nosy? They do nothing but stare at you." After years of facing down locals in numerous cafes and restaurants, we knew what they were going through). Though intensely curious, the adults were too shy to talk and dispatched their children—whose knowledge of the English language they greatly overestimated—to quiz us about where we came from. Watching warily as these would-be young ambassadors skipped across the dance floor to report back, we acknowledged the parents' presence with reassuring waves. After a few drinks had gone down, the night warmed up and uninhibited conversations with all kinds of people sent our heads spinning and flummoxed our interlocutors. On other nights, we would have a go at the energetic, bouncy kind of waltzing they all do, but not this time. We had covered enough ground already.

As the years passed, there were times when differences of opinion with neighbors meant we saw less of them, but reconciliation was always guaranteed at *festas*. Within a few miles of our house are four *lugares* or hamlets which hold their own, paid for by local subscription and reliant on the voluntary activity of a handful of people; our neighbors attend them all and go farther afield as well. For the small farmers, '*lavradores*,' of the Minho, *festas* have always been an opportunity to get away from the backbreaking labor of the farm and enjoy themselves once in a while. They are a chance to make business deals with other farmers and feed merchants and sometimes settle old scores with villagers after quarrels over land ownership, the cause of some bitter disagreements.

Whether Minho farmers are at home, working abroad, or simply migrating for work with the seasons, the tradition is for the wife or *lavradeira* to do the bulk of the land work, as well as bring up children and tend animals. For her, *festas* are a rare opportunity to have some time for herself and a quiet word with her saint. For teenagers, they're an opportunity to get the girl or boy of their dreams in their arms on the dance floor, often a first step to marriage and a farm of one's own. With all these stored-up expectations, it's not surprising that *festas populares* are emotionally charged and sometimes end in tears and, even after a night's partying, the animals still need attention at first light the following morning.

Miguel Torga (1907-1995) was a doctor, poet, and chronicler of village life in Trás-os-Montes in northeastern Portugal, a region known for its rugged individualism. One of his stories is about a single family's disillusionment. Intending to use the occasion to settle an old score with the braggart Marcelino, a husband Nobre wins the fistfight, but at the expense of broken ribs. Seeking a blessing from her tutelary saint, his wife Lucia kneels to open her heart to the image's glassy-eyed gaze, but succeeds only in grazing her knees on the rough ground. Waking to a cold clear dawn surrounded by the detritus of the night's excesses, she feels: "an emptiness in her soul, like that of a tenant just after having paid his rent." Their teenage daughter, Otilia, loses her virginity behind a boulder which, come morning, she could no longer even identify: "In the sanguine faces of those who had covered many miles to get there, there was now the pallor of disillusionment and unconfessed regret."

The next day there was folk music, which traditionally takes place on the more staid Sunday afternoon. After the excesses of the previous night, the villagers reappeared a little subdued in their Sunday best to see a folk group or *rancho* perform. It began with mostly young couples in traditional dress walking hand in hand into the area set aside for dancing, led by, one of their number carrying a banner emblazoned with the group's insignia. There were a dozen dancers, dressed in traditional costume: men in embroidered white shirts, woolen waistcoats with black trousers, and a red sash around the waist; embroidered blouses, full skirts, and white stockings for the women. Performing in pairs, they twirled 'round beside their partners with arms raised above heads, accompanied by that polyphonous singing and accordion playing.

Truly an idiosyncratic form, especially the high-pitched shrieking sound of the female singer. The lyrics come from the pastoral life of the Minho: songs about the maize cycle, sowing, tilling, harvesting, and the stripping and milling of corn. They would have been sung by women in the fields, on their way to and from work and by seated groups stripping corncobs in the farmyard. Today, there is no singing coming from the fields because teams of women no longer work the land but, when I was talking to a neighbor on the road, a tractor went by with a group in the trailer singing at the top of their voices. *Trabalhadoras* said my companion approvingly, indicating there was something special about a party of women bursting into song on their way home from work. I knew what he meant as they certainly sounded special to me. As for stripping corncobs, we have often seen a cluster of women sitting on the roadside outside our neighbor Sandrina's house, stalks piling up beside them, and although we never hear their voices raised in song, they certainly soar in laughter.

Since coming to Portugal, we've been regular attenders at *festas populares* and had some great evenings in amusing company, but there's a side to them that always makes me uneasy. Coming from a Protestant tradition where the sacred and profane were kept well apart, the seamless switching from piety to abandon can be rather unsettling. I always find myself holding back a bit, wary of being carried away by the prevalent mood, which sometimes approaches delirium. Late at night, the throbbing music from the loudspeakers, the flashing lights and the noise of an excitable crowd is reminiscent of "wakes week" in the Lancashire mill town where I was brought up. Like every other child, I was brimming with excitement when the fun fair came to town, yet there was something about all this frenzy of activity that set my spine tingling. It may have been a fear of being led like Pinocchio into a sinister world of make-believe by the bold-faced animals on the Noah's Ark or drawn into danger by the reckless gypsy boys leaping from car to car on the dodgems. Whatever it was, it stayed with me and resurfaced with my first festa popular. Perhaps it's this frisson that attracted me in the first place and kept me going again and again.

Saramago, José. *Journey to Portugal.* London: Harvill Press, 2000.

Torga, Miguel. *Tales & More Tales from the Mountain.* Manchester: Carcanet Press, 1995.

LADIES SPECIAL

Namrata Poddar

As the ladies' special fast train approaches Churchgate, the crowd moves closer to the edge of the platform. We move closer too. We align our bodies in the direction of the train's movement, sprint and step inside before the dust-covered metallic beast trudges to a stop.

This is one of the first things you learn about taking a 6:00 p.m. ladies' special. Climbing into a moving train—your only way to assure a seat. We're pros, not a single sprain or fracture in the last fifteen years, not even in the monsoons.

Inside, I grab a window seat; Carol follows and slides toward me. Within seconds, all seats are taken.

Carol works at Deutsche Bank and walks to Churchgate station every day. I'm a travel agent for Globetrotter at Marine Lines, the stop that comes after Churchgate, so I do the reverse journey first. I take a slow train to Churchgate and then catch the Virar fast that passes through Marine Lines without stopping there. That way, I'm almost sure to get a seat. And Carol's company over the long commute—our only down time to share a heart-to-heart.

The extra commute gets on my nerves sometimes. Especially in summer months when I'm doing double-duty ticketing at work, sending rich college kids backpacking in Europe, all eager to live their Bollywood adventure, get plastered, get laid. But then, I remember Fatima, our other train buddy. "Would *kill* to have a seat for myself. Tilt my head against the window and nap over commutes. I'd be so much productive like that," she tells me often. Productive, that's her favorite word since she's started working at Runway Shoes in Dadar, a few stops north of Churchgate.

A blonde woman climbs into the train. She looks around and occupies the nook splitting the row of seats opposite us. Her head almost touches the metal rack where passengers have kept their carry bags, handbags, umbrellas, groceries. The blonde brings her henna-tattooed hands closer to her chest and starts reading a book. The cover displays a collage of images— Queen's Necklace bordering a little too blue Arabian Sea, an endless skyline with Ambani residence highlighted in gold, the call centers at Bandra-Kurla complex, and a group of half-naked women dancing on a stage. I lean forward but don't see any of the guide names I know. No *Lonely Planet* logo either. From the title hiding in the corner, it looks like a tourist guide in a foreign language. Mumbai written in blood red stands bold above the images.

By the time the train stops at Dadar, the compartment is so full we wonder if Fatima will be able to climb in. We crane our necks toward the exit door. No sign of her.

The train moves again. The shrill grinding of the metallic wheels blends with the drone of the fans on our compartment's ceiling. A rancid air adds to the stuffiness inside.

The women standing closer to the gate twitch; a couple of them scream at the fisherwoman who has sandwiched herself between two passengers. She is forcing her way forward while trying to balance a huge basket of fish on her head. Droplets of water trickle through.

"You're moving to the luggage compartment next stop or I'll call the police!" One of the women says, as she squints and brings her handkerchief to her nose.

"Train belong to your old man or what?" the fisherwoman yells. Few women grumble. Voices back and forth.

"The luggage compartment is full, can't you see?"

"The next train was to come in five minutes, couldn't you

wait?"

"Why should *I* wait when none of *you* do?"

"The stink from that water on my sari! Aiiyoh, even Surf Ultra can't wash this away."

"Royalty should take first class then." The fisherwoman gives her basket a deliberate shake. The women around squeal and duck their heads.

I remove a cutting board from my bag and place it on my lap. "Drama *every* day." I shake my head and start chopping carrots. A little kitchen work on the return commute goes a long way. I get done with dinner and cleaning at home earlier and can help my children with homework before bed. Productive, Fatima would say.

Carol returns fifty rupees in change to the aunty seated across. "I'll bring you the red ones tomorrow," she says as she offers aunty a couple of yellow and green water bottles. Aunty is Carol's regular customer for Tupperware—a side business she runs over the train rides.

"Excuse me," a voice repeats in the distance, sounding more like *scuuz me*. Carol looks at me, a sparkle in her eyes. We love Fatima's town accent since she's starting working at Runway. Fatima pushes past the crowd and plods toward us, panting for breath. We also love the fit-flop she is wearing these days with fake jadau buttons on the straps. Stylish, yet functional, and the best part, Runway employees get 75% discount. If only we had her shoe size.

Carol pushes her bag of Tupperware products on the luggage rack above, next to her purse. Fatima sits on her lap. We hi-hello, complain about the heat, catch up on our day, and vent about Wednesday, Sunday still an eternity away. We fan ourselves—Fatima with the bottom of her tunic, Carol with a newspaper, and I, with my palm every few seconds I stop chopping veggies.

"What news on the building, babes?" Fatima says,

flashing her new vocabulary again. The girls know I was at my residential society's meeting yesterday. My building is to go for redevelopment like many others in our neighborhood. The three-stories will be demolished and a twelve-story tower will be put up in place. My family will get an extra room like other residents if we all accept the terms set in the construction contractor's agreement.

"Same old. The hag refuses to give in." I empty chopped carrots in a Tupperware box to make room for radish. "Always one sample in the herd." The hag is my building's oldest resident, a widow unwilling to move and rent elsewhere for two years like the rest of us while the contractor builds a new tower.

Carol rubs my upper arm. The girls know how much I want the bigger space, especially with twins born to my brother. "A family of eight living in one-bedroom flat. Like being stuck in this fucking train compartment for good," I mutter, avoiding eye contact with the girls. Truth is—five years have passed with these meetings and I don't want to make-believe any more, nod every time I share my building drama with them. Give it time, *babes.* What else will they say?

Our heads bob to the rhythm of the train's movement. Another train rushes past ours, the screech of its wheels drowning all noise in our compartment. When the train disappears, glass-covered high-rises in the distance loom over three to four story buildings like mine where black snakes of tar paint cover the outer walls to prevent monsoon water from leaking in. A long, wide gutter connects Bombay to Mumbai.

"Aa." Carol pokes my knee with her index finger. The women in our side of the compartment have started playing Antakshari. It's Carol's turn to sing a movie song beginning with A. *Ae dil hain mushkil jeena yahan*, she begins, bringing her shoulder to playfully pat mine. Fatima and aunty join the singing, clapping hands in my direction. I force a smile and join the others. In this collective effort to music, the heat in the compartment dissipates.

Andheri approaches. Many women get down. Few climb in. Air at last.

Two women enter. One is wearing a black pencil skirt, a gray shirt, and a red printed silk scarf wrapped around her neck; another is wearing a navy blue shirt dress and her dark gelled hair is pulled back into a sleek ponytail. They sit in the row next to ours. The blond is sitting opposite them, the Mumbai guide still in her hands.

The sun sets outside. Sunrays light up the brochures stuck on the compartment walls—abortion ads, contraception ads, English training and grooming school ads, home loan ads, and 999 number ads—police escorts you can call during late night and early morning commutes. This latter, since the Delhi rape incident. One brochure dominates the rest though, covering the sides of the walls, including corners below the metal racks holding passenger bags. Next to the face of a meditating Shiva, the cell phone number of a gold-medalist Baba who assures a 100% wish fulfillment to all desires—higher salary, fertility issues, soul mate search, mental or physical illness. His Facebook page and WhatsApp contact are listed below too.

I'm singing with the girls, *yeh hain Bombay meri jaan*, as I continue chopping French beans on my lap. Below Baba's brochure, the blond and the two women who just got in are leaning toward each other, chitchatting, laughing. The woman with the silk scarf brings her finger to point something inside the blonde's tourist guide. The woman in the shirtdress types something into her iPhone and nods at them. A Louis Vuitton bag hangs by the woman's shoulder, the one who's wearing the shirtdress. The fingers tapping her iPhone sport perfectly manicured, scarlet nails.

I stare at the meditating Shiva controlling the walls of our train, his third eye closed over a blissful smile, and give a shriek so loud, the live chorus in front stops. In reflex, I take the finger in my mouth. Aunty gives a gasp and turns her head away. I look down at my cutting board and notice a sea of blood where chopped green beans have formed a pretty archipelago. The islands have sprawled outward leaving a rectangular hollow in the center. The map reminds me of the shriveled back cover of a travel guide on my city I've seen at Globetrotter's. Only senior employees can access the bookcase where the collector's copy stands tall, locked away, turning its back on us. As I taste the sweet sourness of my blood, I wonder what stories fill up the pages of the antique guide? What color the cover page must have used to name the ancient archipelago? And which name?

ODE TO THE INDIGENOUS

Gina Ferrara

After the city slipped and became a wound
without a tourniquet, bleeding old
with the new no one knew,
the treasures like the indigenous,
where the crepe myrtles grew
from south to north, the magenta, lavender,
pink and white in tandem
and clustered looking bleach barked, barely
bending towards the lake…summer,
the scent of brine and the bridge lights
illuminated, smaller than pinpricks in shades of amber
for twenty five miles before the horizon,
the point with the darkened lighthouse,
splashy staccato, jagged rocks breaking waves,
the big tree in the park, just beyond the labyrinth,
the bend in the distance where we sat watching
vessels pass with faded letters and foreign flags,
tankers carrying barrels and grain flanked by tugboats,
how the cicadas signaled the start of imminent Augusts and
Septembers
without being seen from the apexes of oaks.

WHAT SETTLES AFTER THE STARS
Robert Mangeot

The receptionist at Maison Vulpeque asked what brought me to Reims, and I almost blurted the dead monks were out to get me. They were, of course, those shorn and vengeful bastards. Even so, I couldn't risk saying "dead monks" out loud, no one could, not and land a ticket down where those monks surely haunted the champagne caves.

"Tasting," I said too loudly. My voice echoed across the lobby, deserted for off-season. "I'd very much enjoy a tasting."

"Ah, excellent! Here we have the finest in La Champagne." She basked in the idea a moment. "So, one for the tour?"

I nodded by degrees, worried the twitchier version I fought would shake loose a bead of sweat or, worse, my fake mustache. I was persona non grata here, since my column mentioned their flagship label Anserre evoked all the passion of kissing a rich aunt. Hence the mustache, and a wig to cover the signature sheen of my scalp. Carl Haplinger of *Haplinger's Guide to Sparkling Wine* and, recently, of *Vino Veritas* magazine, of countless hair-challenged headshots and personal appearances, sporting a mop-top and handlebar? No one would guess it.

The receptionist took my twelve euros and went about assembling the paperwork. So as not to hover, I paced the swank gleam of the lobby. *The gleam of a swindler's eye*, reflex begged me to write. Precisely the sort of line that got me a monk's curse. Across the marble tile, flanked by art nouveau fashionista posters and spotlit magnums, beckoned the oak doors that led to the caves.

She slid over my ticket. I was in. Maison Vulpeque,

Champagne's *grand marque* of *grand marques*, their wines first plucked, stomped, and fermented centuries ago by those blasted monks. If there could be peace, peace would be brokered here. "As if carrying on from the monks," I'd written once of Anserre, "at a hundred bucks, it pairs well with a vow of poverty." Soon afterward, my taste buds started going in and out like faulty wiring, a nuisance become a demon. As of this dismal afternoon, I'd tasted nothing but metallic ash for a month. The doctors swore it was gastrointestinal, manageable if not yet managed. No, it was the monks. What brought me to Reims was surrender.

The desk phone bleated as if on a rising note of alarm. The receptionist picked up and listened. Her look my way soured into a *j'accuse*.

She cupped a hand over the receiver. "I am sorry," she said, not sounding it, "but there has been a mistake. Today we are sold out."

Around the lobby I counted myself and her and the art nouveau ladies in their poster frames. "Sold out?"

"Completely. Booked all the day."

"But I have a ticket."

She produced my twelve euros atop her desk. "Yes, I will need that back, Monsieur Haplinger."

Damn and double damn. "You don't understand. It's urgent."

Apparently she didn't feel the need to understand, and neither did the security guard she summoned. Clamping onto my other arm was Jean-Pierre Vulpeque himself, stylishly dressed and flinty-eyed, and together the men hustled me out onto Rue du Champ-de-Mars.

"Please," I said, "I need in the caves. Just for a second."

Jean-Pierre assessed me as he might a rot on his grapes. "You wrote we bottle extortion with a hint of jam."

"For which *Grand Cru* dubbed me a braying American ass.

All in good fun."

"Our wines, Monsieur, are only for those of taste."

I froze. Lacking taste had been lobbed at me by countless wine growers, readers, and the oddly monkish street person who harassed me outside my building. I'd heard it, too, from the psychic who ran off with my ex-wife, but as clearly he got the notion from her, I'd dismissed it as a message from the spirit world. Now, I glimpsed the full depths of the plot against me. My mind reeled with visions of Jean-Luc in the maison's crypts and chanting the monks upon me.

I trudged back for the hotel. My ramble took me through *centre ville,* past the showroom compounds of champagne royalty clean and bright amid gritty Reims. Each chateau, like a dragon atop its treasure, squatted upon kilometers of chalk caves, each cave layered with racks of champagne aging in the cold and dark. In the hush between street noises, I could almost hear the monks down there laughing.

At the hotel bar, I ordered a ratafia, the brandy made from leftover grapes. I didn't taste the hard stuff any better, but at least its embers burned in my stomach. I sipped, and in rushed filed-away memories of past brandies—better ones—my brain cells firing like tiny phantom limbs. Surely, there would be excess wood smoke and cloying raisin.

There was a sucker born every vintage. I'd written that about Anserre, and the French howled blue murder. Comments and letters surged, topping even the monthly haul for Wynndi, the model-turned-foodie adventurer. The more creatively I flogged champagne's nosebleed prices, say as highway snobbery, the more cheers and protests flooded in, the more the French returned fire, the more it had built Carl Haplinger, bad boy bon vivant.

One ratafia became two, and two became courage. A short trundle later, I stood beside the greeter stand at Le Comptoir d'Or, the home brasserie of gourmand Marc Balustre. He owed me, whether he'd admit it or not. He'd only broken through to B-list after he devoted his column in *Grand Cru* to lambasting mine in *Vino Veritas*. "Haplinger couldn't choose a wine to christen a ship" was his go-to jibe. The monks had made certain of it.

Oh, Marc saw me just fine there at his fern, Marc wearing his too-tight apron and a snarl. He had to seat me—I was that famous—but he didn't have to make it snappy. I wasn't *that* famous.

A junior waiter deposited me at a table by the kitchen. No bread arrived, no water, and I sat enduring the stares of the tourist set. Victim of my own success, that was what I'd become. Turn of phrase had launched me from piecework fluff to dinner parties, charity auctions and socialite divorcées, from hand-to-mouth freelancing to the must-read column on sparkling wine. I'd slept with Wynndi. Only the once, but still!

In time, Marc brought my ratafia and slapped a menu on the table. "Tonight we have a monkfish casserole. For apéritif I suggest a fine champagne, though you will think it priced to shame a blackmailer."

"What did you say?"

"Blackmailer. It was you who said this of my cousin's Brut Reserve."

"No, you have monkfish tonight?"

"In a saffron broth."

Monkfish: fate's casserole. "I need your help, wine man to wine man."

"You? Hah!"

"I'm out, Marc. Done."

He drew up straight. "Out how?"

"At *Vino Veritas*. As of last month, I'm special features only. Except, they haven't assigned a feature yet."

No more than I deserved, his sniff seemed to say, but after my deep pull of brandy, his air of victory evaporated. "What cause did they give?"

I could have said my editor had long grown suspicious of my ever more erratic tasting notes, how she had interns check my adjectives. I could have said reader mail had skewed of late toward threats of bodily harm over ruined weddings and romantic getaways. Sales of *Haplinger's Guide* had ebbed to where the next edition might be digital only, stripped of coffee table book status. All symptoms of the deeper truth.

"The dead monks," I said. "They've cursed me."

Bound to happen, his next sniff seemed to add. Bound to happen.

After closing, we drank ratafia and I told Marc about that street person with patchy hair and a poncho who'd chased me down Gansevoort Street—"no taste!" he'd cackled. How I'd spent a month officially staring into the abyss. Staring back was a dead monk brandishing a bottle.

"So," Marc said, "I am to intercede, yes?"

"It's just you're a respected figure about Reims. And you buy Anserre by the truckload."

"To apologize, this is a most good thing. But your regret must be sincere."

"Look at me. I'm a wreck."

He peered over his snifter at me.

"I don't know why they have it in for me," I said. "Yes, I stirred the pot. And Vulpeque ladled all the way to the bank."

Marc savored his ratafia. "The stars."

"What?"

"One night, long ago, the great Dom Pérignon, after a life dedicated to his cellars, he samples the first champagne and he cries out, 'Brothers! Come quickly! I am drinking the stars!'"

"Pérignon. I'll bet he's the ringleader."

"Champagne is of the heavens, and you call it a whore."

I coughed a brandied cough. I'd been particularly proud of that column, deeming some new vintage as yet another French prostitute: a high-priced headache, and she and your cash were gone come morning.

"Well, there are cheaper wines."

"You may tell them this at Vulpeque yourself."

"Hold on. It was a game, that's all. Someone ought to jab at hundred-dollar bottles, shouldn't they?"

"And you believe the monks think champagne a game?"

"I'm through with it, whatever they think." I stomped to roust the monks in their caves. "You win, brothers. You win."

Marc agreed to make inquiries come morning, if I promised to dwell that night on my situation, which I did, and to stay clear of Vulpeque, which I didn't. The monks dogged me from the moment I dropped into bed. On the back of my eyelids, dour men in dark robes seeped out from their caves and cranked up their wine presses. After a bland croissant and coffee for breakfast, I was dodging the early tour buses outside the maison's stucco walls. Above me, the day turned an intense blue. A French blue. The air simmered with a great gathering of spiritual forces. Judgment at hand.

Except, Marc neither called nor returned my voicemails, and my roaming turned further afield. Soon the grand compounds were some blocks behind me. Hard to say how many, given I'd become lost in the zigzag of backstreets. Doubling back, I stumbled upon a timeworn villa of dingy sandstone and barred windows, its wrought-iron fence topped with spikes fit for displaying heads. Its sign warned: *Chateau Des Mendiants.* The House of the Monks.

Over the years, I'd sprayed zingers at every house in Champagne worth the spray, or so I thought. Either Mendiants was new on the scene or these were the gears of fate in motion. I needed a hard blink to spot a dark-haired woman of about fifty in the gravel courtyard, smoking meditatively. She said, "You want to taste?"

"You have no idea."

She stubbed out her cigarette, flowed past a gray cat dozing in the sun, and vanished inside the chateau. There was nothing for it now but to give what pounds of flesh the monks demanded. In case this might be my last known location, I texted Marc my plan and angled through the compound gate.

The cat did not give way. I shuffled around it and into a tidy foyer decked out with photos of the woman and what had to be the husband posing in this or that vineyard. I found her banging around in a living room converted to a makeshift bar. She introduced herself as Elodie, and she presented a flight of champagnes arranged from sweet to dry. The rosé came first, its foam the color of watered-down blood.

I watched its bubbles roil. "I expected monks."

"Okay."

"Not live ones." I leaned in conspiratorially. "I'm Carl Haplinger."

"Hello, Carl." She topped off my rosé and began reciting the property's winemaking heritage back to a monastery on these grounds, how she remained committed to the old methods. In front of me the champagne fizzed away, an invitation or a dare. I gave it a swirl and quaffed it, wet and ashen down my throat.

Elodie said, "Okay."

Very well then. The monks might have snuffed out tasting their wine, but there wasn't a blessed thing they could do to stop my getting good and drunk on it. I plowed through a cuvée and a Blanc de Noirs and informed Elodie she could keep them coming. She did, and with no other business around, she brought out a flute for herself.

"Where's your husband?" I asked. "Let's make it a party."

"Dead."

"That's awful."

"Yes. Too sad. But is this not the way of things? They go on. Every day the sun and the moon."

While we drank, she talked of her husband and their dream

of running a winery, how they had taken early retirement and bought this tumbledown villa, so renamed Mendiant as a monastic money trap. He passed away before their first pressing. She had buried him and forged on alone through the blending, the aging and, now after years, the pouring.

We were deep into the Blanc de Noirs, me explaining about the monks, when in my swirl I caught Marc there, trading pecks with Elodie. He plopped on the next stool and made a show of sniffing the champagne.

"What about at Vulpeque?" I said.

"We must give them time. After the fake mustache, Jean-Pierre is doubly suspicious."

"Tell them I take it all back. Everything. I'll make a sacrifice." I slumped in Elodie's direction. "Could I trouble you for a goat?"

She laughed, and not the good-idea-let's-offer-up-a-goat kind, either. "You have the stress."

"Says you and a bunch of quack doctors. Here's a surefire cause of stress: a curse from beyond the grave."

"No goats."

"You're right. Too bloody. It's not like I sliced open a Benedictine, did I?"

Marc said, "Take them a ham."

"They'll like that?"

Elodie blew out her lips. "Enough, yes? You need a cave? I have a cave."

A flutter washed over me. Over Marc too, by his sudden suck of air. If you believed in dead monks avenging the slightest slight to champagne, Elodie's theory went, then any champagne cave should be as good as the next. She made the fatefully perfect sense that only ever came with heavy drinking.

We took a flashlight, a chilled Blanc de Noirs, and a cold sandwich plate out toward a stone outbuilding. The sun had dipped below the horizon, and the moon hung fixed in a smoky-blue sky. Elodie unlatched the outbuilding and shepherded us into a varnished A-frame of tasting counters and souvenir barware. Along the back wall, a stairwell plunged below ground. There, shrouded in gloom, waited the cave.

Marc gripped my shoulder and wished me *bon chance*. Elodie clunked and clanked the cellar door open and issued me the wine and sandwiches. I drew a stale breath and, with prodding, wobbled down spiral stairs cut into the chalk. Finally, however many circles Dante would put me beneath Reims, I felt my way out into a passage spared from pitch-black by emergency lights. Ahead ran a straight-shot corridor with a rough masonry arch grazing my scalp. My eyes adjusted to the murk, and I could make out racks of bottles riddling, then whole antechambers of racks melting off into darkness. Elodie had been spot on: this looked as good a place as any to encounter a dead monk.

I edged further inside. "All right, here I am." My voice burst through the corridor and washed back over me, dying as it passed. No ghostly wails broke the quiet. "I brought a nice Blanc de Noirs. And sandwiches. Cold beef."

No wisps through the spider webs. No spectral moans.

I wrestled open the champagne. The pop of the cork echoed and faded. Not even a rattle of glass.

"You want to see me suffer, is that it?" I saluted them with the Blanc de Noirs. "Santé."

I guzzled long and hard from the bottle, wine trickling off my chin. It might have been champagne or formaldehyde, for all I tasted. If the monks appreciated the gesture, they didn't show it. I eased down to the floor, shadows curling around me, and between swigs and cold beef, I told whoever haunted the place about the rise and fall of Carl Haplinger. The pittance-per-word freelancer, the jolt of celebrity, the social gadfly, the bridezillas, and the agonizing loss of taste. The damndest thing dawned on me: I wasn't sorry. I had slept with an ex-model.

Flabby and hairless Carl…in bed with a former cover girl. It was simple, really: no monks, no champagne, no hell of a run.

"Thank you," I called out.

The words rolled around and off into the blackness. No monks dead or alive emerged to argue the point. That was that, then. I made it to my feet and hobbled for the stairs. Like Elodie said, things went on. I toasted the idea with champagne copper-ash on my tongue. Old coins, that was how I'd have written the taste. Old coins with stardust on the finish.

DEEPER IN

Christina Selby

We pulled into a small parking lot off the only road that stretched through the wilderness of South Dakota's Badlands. We had spent the day languidly driving through the park, awestruck by the otherworldly landscape of buttes and bluffs. In the diagonal light before dusk, the gray-white mounds turned golden yellow, scored with rose and tangerine bands.

This was the first week of a six-month couch-surfing, car-camping road trip with my new enterprising boyfriend. Our plan was to tour the entire western United States doing research for a non-profit we intended to start together. We had whittled down all our possessions to what we could pack into a VW Jetta.

Introduced by a mutual friend, we had become acquainted via email. He, typing from Paris, and me, from Milwaukee. After bonding over a concern for the state of the earth, he invited me to join him in his oversized Parisian loft to help file the non-profit paperwork while he finished out his commitments. Under the influence of the city of romance, we quickly fell in love. For two months, we dined on French cuisine, frequented fantastic clubs, and admired painters' creations as we walked along the Seine and through open-air markets where flowers perfumed the air. We showered daily, wore fashionable clothes, and used the bathroom with the door closed. It was like we were on an extended honeymoon.

When we left Paris to embark on our road trip, a new phase of our relationship unfolded. An intimate familiarity between us grew from being together in an enclosed space for days on end. After a week on the road, the car smelled of gas station food ground into car mats and dirty clothes infused with campfire smoke and lake water.

Despite the lack of privacy, I was still working to put my best self forward and keep my gory insides under wraps. A tall order with no door behind which I could hide my bodily functions, as we all prefer to do at the beginning of relationships. My friend, Emily, the one who introduced us, kept her guys believing for at least the first six months of a new relationship that she magically did not poop.

Despite my efforts at concealment, my raw humanity was leaking out. The veil of romance that enchanted us in Paris was lifting. I had reached that moment in a relationship when I start asking myself questions like: can I live with the smell of this person's morning breath for the rest of my life?

As the sun was touching down on the horizon, we hopped out of the car and walked through a grassy meadow into arid terrain looking for a camp spot. Only one other car was in the parking lot. It seemed odd to me that so few visitors were in the park in July. Maybe they knew something we didn't.

Pressed for daylight, we jogged past a sign warning BEWARE OF RATTLESNAKES with a black-and-white drawing of a large, ominous rattler beneath. The dominance of erosion was apparent on the geography where wind and water wore down the landscape's resolve over the ages. We shuffled over ground covered in the chalky sand and broken-up rocks that fell from the buttes. We found a private camping spot on the far side of two small buttes buffered from any road noise. On the edge of a bluff overlooking the expanse, the badlands stretched for miles in front of us. Perfect, we agreed.

We worked together to set up the dome tent New Boyfriend picked up at a sporting goods store. It was a car camping luxury tent, large and roomy enough for us to stand in. Pounding tent stakes in with large rocks, we managed only to bend them when the firm ground refused their entry.

"Ground's too hard. Let's just pile a few rocks on the loops to hold the rainfly down," New Boyfriend said.

We watched a herd of bison grazing on short-grass prairie on the other side of the chasm. A bighorn sheep eased its way over rocky outcrops, its cloven hoofs clacking on the slopes. The last light of day faded from the sky and washed the buttes clean of color. New Boyfriend and I lingered outside as the sky blackened into a moonless night. The hazy Milky Way rose from the horizon into the darkness above. Stars stretched deeper into space than either of us had seen before.

Without a fire, the cool night seeped into my bones. Fast moving clouds obscured the stars on the distant horizon. We retired to our tent and slipped into warm sleeping bags. Lying next to each other, we listened to the silence of the barren landscape as sleep overcame us.

Crashing thunder rang in my ears and startled me awake. Drips of water hit my face. In the darkness I could make out New Boyfriend sitting upright with his arms outstretched as if performing an odd prayer.

"What's going on? Are you okay?" I said.

"Serious storm. The wind keeps blowing the tent over and rain's coming in through the window," he shouted over rumbling thunder. "I'm getting soaked trying to hold it up."

"It's getting wet over here too," I said. Lightning struck nearby, shaking the ground and lighting the tent. The air had the peculiar ozone smell of electricity in motion. Grasping the power of the storm on the other side of the flimsy nylon walls, panic started pulsing through my body.

"Holy crap, that was close!" I shrieked.

"It's all right, it will pass," he said.

"Maybe we should go back to the car. I heard that if you get struck by lightning in a car, the wheels absorb the electricity," I said, suddenly wanting to be anywhere but there.

"Yah, that's a myth. As long as you don't touch anything when lightning strikes, the electricity dissipates from the body of the car. Doesn't have to do with the wheels." He was working hard to hold up the tent, which violent winds were now threatening to fold in half.

"Ugh! We don't have a flashlight, remember? Even with the sky lighting up like this, it's too dark to find our way back," I said.

"We'd be lightning rods standing out there in the open anyway," he replied.

I nodded, wiping rain from my face with my flimsy t-shirt.

"If I don't hold up these poles, they'll snap. Then, likely, the wind will blow us right over the bluff. But I might get struck by lightning, holding onto metal like this in an electrical storm." He was way too calm, talking about the ways he might die in the night.

"I guess the rocks didn't work," I said. He craned his neck and shot me a glance that said *not helpful.* "Doesn't matter," I backpedaled.

My mind was closing in on itself from fear. "We have to stay away from tall trees," I mumbled, remembering the advice of an outdoor guide I once camped with.

"Good thing there are no trees out here...at all." He was looking at me, wondering if I was losing it.

Think, think, I thought, exhaling hard to reign in my panic. "What if you put your shoes on and hold up the poles with your feet. The rubber soles will keep the lightning from burning through you." Worth a try, I thought.

He eyed me dubiously, but decided going along with me would calm me down. "Okay. Throw me my shoes. I'll try it." He secured the tent poles lying on his back with his shoes up in the air.

"Grab your shoes, too. Help me hold up your side of the tent," he said motioning with his chin.

"Okay," I said, wiggling out of my sleeping bag.

Trapped between being blown 200 feet over a bluff and getting struck by lightning, we lay next to each other, hands and feet in the air and thighs pressed against our bellies for support.

Then, whether I let my guard down because of sheer exhaustion or due to the fact that I was lying in what in yoga class we call the "wind-relieving pose," I farted. Even the noise of the storm couldn't conceal it. I scrunched my face up in embarrassment.

Great, I thought, just let it all hang out—panic, losing it, and now this! Our journey together had taken us from flower-perfumed Parisian markets to fart-sealed tents in only a few short months. Here is where our romance has come to die.

"Must be those damn barking spiders," he offered. "They follow me around relentlessly." And then, in a gesture of solidarity, he farted, too. We looked at each other sideways and giggled. It was not a terribly romantic moment. But in the place of romance, I realized, something deeper was rising up. A more intimate, real, and yes, smellier relationship was blossoming.

"We look like fried possums," he said.

"At least we'll fry together," I said, still giggling, my panic dissipating. I curled against him and dropped my legs—one unanticipated gas release was enough for the moment. We stayed like that until the howling winds began to subside and we fell into an exhausted, soggy sleep.

The blazing sun woke us a couple hours later. Hot sunbeams pierced through the tears the storm left in our tent walls, spearing my skin like lasers. We dragged our wet sleeping bags back to the car in the light of day and threw the tent into the first trash can we found.

"Wait," said New Boyfriend, "let's keep the bottom, we can use it as a tarp."

After that, we relaxed into our road trip and each other. We wouldn't face a storm of that size or force again. But just in case, we invested in a low-to-the-ground four-season tent with sturdy poles, trading in the idea of a luxury dome for functionality.

Our journey together stretched from months into years, and New Boyfriend turned into Long-term Husband, to whom I am still happily married. Although we've seen some storms in our relationship over the years, none have been quite like the one that knocked us out of new relationship bliss and into a real life together. Storms these days, after ten years together, are fewer and father in between.

ARTEMIS

Ashley Mace Havird

We had to swerve to miss her.
Tattered mules, blue bathrobe trailing
the pavement, cheese pie half-eaten,
white hair electric in the Sahara winds—
surely she had given the slip to her sitter
in one of the crumbling neoclassical mansions
Artemonas is famous for.

We were hunting the prize of the island,
a wooden icon of Virgin and Child.
(The story pure romance: a golden stream
in the sea, and there, floating,
the miracle—the fishermen blessed.)
On Sifnos, an island that boasts
a blue-domed church "for every day
of the year," *the* one was not so easy to find.
But find we finally did. Amid lingering incense,
a gaudy silver panel with holes that yielded
tiny sea-black mummy-faces.

Leaving, we saw her again—this time
for who she was. Dressed as a man,
in boots and cotton work shirt,
trousers bunched at the waist—Artemis
took the center of the one road
from Artemonas to (where else?) Apollonia.
Cigarette clamped between lips,

she was off to complain (it seemed plain)
over a thimbleful of thick coffee
to her brother, that old sun-god.
She has no use for Little Raisin-Face
and her shriveled thumbprint of a Son:
What were they but keyholes in that fancy door?

Why did people seek *that* virgin, anyway,
with her droning litanies, her suffocating
incense… Then again, who could afford
a decent quiver of arrows nowadays?
No game anymore, unless you want pigeon.

UNSQUARED

Bill Cole

If I wrote a blog this would be it, but I don't write a blog. I don't even have a computer. I am told what is occurring up north in the streets of Cairo is revolution, that Tahrir Square is a launching pad for soaring heights and realized ambitions. Demands are being hurled through the air: *Bread, Freedom, Social Justice*. All the result of social media. That is what I am told. The considerable technological skills of young people have allowed grievances to connect, actions to coalesce. I am told all of this, but I don't own a computer, so I have to trust my ears, have to trust the lips of others.

Everything that is happening, I am told, is due to young people and their cyber skills. I am 14. That's young. I don't have a computer, though. No computer, no skills. If I want to see an actual computer, I can go to my friend Atef's home. His family has a computer. Only some of the families here have a computer.

We do not live in Cairo where most of the people cohabitate with their fancy machines and their virtual ether. We are not in Alexandria where they flaunt their textured artistic tastes. We just exist in our little village in Upper Egypt, quite near the Nile, a bunch of struggling people with no Internet service who are simply told about an uprising taking place, a fight for Bread, Freedom, Social Justice. How excellent that news sounds. But many of us are not feeling much of any of it because we don't have computers. We are blind to the eye of the storm, and the eye of storm is blind to us. I don't understand how it can all happen with so many different goals tangled together.

The Brotherhood wants change so they can make an Islamic state out of us, the laborers want change so they can get paid a fair wage, the women want change so they can be treated with respect, the younger generation wants change so they can have a future. It seems too much at once. Throw two or three balls in the air, there is a good chance you can catch them all. Throw ten balls in the air, there is a good chance you will catch none of them. Besides, it seems that to many in Cairo, freedom means being even more like Americans and their European neighbors, eating their hamburgers and speaking and listening on their cell phones. For me, change would not be about getting more. It would be about getting rid of more to live our lives more easily without the corruption that suffocates us.

Atef and I have been talking about getting involved with one of the local youth projects set up to improve the conditions of our village. There are many tasks to choose from, anything from collecting garbage, to distributing bread, to raising money for newly arrived families from the Theban Hills who were squeezed from their homes to make room for more tourism. We are less focused on the broader demands of Tahrir Square and more concerned with the immediate needs of our local community. Ours might be modest efforts, but they can make a big difference in the lives of many of our neighbors.

I often wonder if any of those young people in Tahrir lack a computer in their homes. I suppose I will have to ask someone who can tell me that. Sometimes I think I'm better off looking for answers in the moon.

I do not feel at ease revealing the location of my village. I have fear for my family's safety. Disclosing such information would make us vulnerable to the whims of the police, despite the fact this is not an actual blog nor is it even words typed on a keyboard. It is just an imagining, a tendency, at times, a desire.

We go to school and are told by our teachers to ignore the wayward influence of these machines. We are urged to heed the directive transmitted to Muhammad: *Iqra*. Read. Ingest the text. We are taught we will eventually move past the Western part of the world as long as they remain overly focused on profit and indulgence, but I am told many of our people do not resist these same seductions.

Where we live, time fades into the stillness of our days. We don't feel the moments passing like elephant strides as they do in the West. The hours do not represent monetary units to us. My father worked as a farmer, tending to the barley and sorghum and corn and cotton. He worked long days and wanted only to provide for our family. He told us that when he was younger, the West wrecked our agriculture by using Sadat to push the crops that would make them the most money, leaving the local farmers with next to nothing.

"Once our army joined in with the West's moneymaking schemes, the rape was complete," he said.

Father's heart stopped when I was six. I miss him every day. He used to run his mustache across my cheek like paint brush bristles on a canvas, love as a work of art. This memory buoys me when I struggle to recall the sound of his voice.

I live with my mother, older brother, older sister, and two younger brothers. We have been running a small sandwich shop out of the front part of our home for the past seven years. Our specialty is grilled pigeon with tomato and rice sandwiches. We have a pigeon coop and grow our own tomatoes. My mother, with help from my older sister, prepares the food in the kitchen.

Hamam Mahshi is considered a delicacy throughout our country, but we need to conserve the food we have, so rather than serve stuffed pigeons, we use the meat more sparingly by putting them in sandwiches. People love our sandwiches, but they are getting smaller so that our supply of pita lasts longer. We also sell maps, postcards, and paperweights for the tourists who are more than glad to peek into our local history. When the people living around Tahrir look out their windows, they are reportedly seeing the creation of something fresh and exciting. When we look out our window, we see the same trees tethered to their roots, waving in the breeze.

The police walk by, maniacally pursuing their next opportunity to extort. They stop in routinely for our sandwiches, but they usually don't pay. They often demand we give them money or threaten to close down our shop. They also require more meat in their sandwiches than we usually give our customers. If they don't think there is enough pigeon on their plate, they threaten to arrest my mother. One of them even once opened up his sandwich and pelted her with chunks of pigeon. I have walked in on my mother crying to herself after having these kinds of interactions with them. She always pulls herself together and continues on with her day. Maybe, one day, she won't be able to pull herself together. What then? Our police are crooked and selfish. They are puppets of the regime. I can almost understand why that fruit vendor lit himself on fire in Tunisia last month. It gets to feeling hopeless.

The latest we are being told is that the police have been freeing all of the jailed criminals around Cairo so that they will start attacking the people in Tahrir Square like wild dogs, disrupting any progress the protestors hope to make. In light of this rumor, my older brother, along with several of his friends, have joined a large group of young men who have been organizing a community watch. They are preparing to stand guard at our borders to protect us against any of these runaway prisoners who try to enter our village seeking mischief. I am worried that violence will find by brother. I couldn't handle losing another member of my family, another strong man erased. My mother would surely wither away from such an outcome.

We have a few photo albums in our house. Members of our family posed in some formation or the camera snapping at a moment when nobody is prepared for their picture to be taken.

They are typical photographs, but they never seem to describe what I feel about my life. I think the photographs that would truly reflect my life do not belong to us. Those pictures are scattered across other people's photo albums throughout the world. They are the photographs of tourists posing in front of desired sites while I might have incidentally been caught in the background. A newly married American couple embracing in front of the ancient Mosque while I am trotting, mid-stride, in the photo's upper corner. A family from Canada poses on the banks of the Nile as Atef and I laze on the water behind them, unwittingly, at the edge of the frame. A group of French teenagers lean in front of the ruins as I unknowingly gather stones from the ground nearby, hovering within the image. Of course, I am not aware of the existence of these photos, but if I went through all of the photo albums of all the travelers that passed through my village over the last fourteen years, I am certain there would be many pictures of me stuck somewhere in the background, enough to fill up an entire photo album. That would be a photo album that really captures my life. That would be the type of photo album that would probably summarize most everybody's life: stuck in somewhere in the background.

So many young people say they can't wait to grow up. They anticipate adulthood as the goal to be achieved. So many others never want to grow up. They are convinced their youth preserves the illusion of relative freedom. They think all that blissful innocence rudely changes as they become adults. I don't think it matters either way. Nothing every really changes. It doesn't matter about our age. In school, our teacher tells us how important it is to learn. It will lead us to a bigger life, a better life. I don't believe it. The only ones who have the power to lead us to a better life are the people in charge. Mubarak doesn't want us to have a better life. He only cares about his select group of friends. He wants to keep us living a poor life.

Atef and I are planning to start a punk rock duo. He plays the drums and I am learning how to play this battered bass guitar that used to belong to my brother and is missing a string. My concern is Atef wants to do this with the foolish notion of attracting girls and becoming a celebrity. I want to do it with the purpose of using my unease to construct monuments to my unease. Okay, maybe I want to attract girls a little bit, too.

We all stay pretty much the same. The circumstances surrounding us all stay pretty much the same. Some might call this trapped, but I am not so sure that is accurate. Trapped means there is something better we are being kept from that we cannot reach, but I don't think there is anything waiting for us on some other side. Many of us are led to believe material goods and a more luxurious life are waiting for us on the other side, but these fetishes are just a mirage. They are not even signs of an improved life, just an empty obsession with the West. I do catch myself wondering if this moment in this place will be somehow different. Maybe the army is finally with the people and Mubarak will be removed tomorrow. Then again, maybe Mubarak will still be in power 200 years from now, another living relic, another pharaoh.

The fact that nothing changes can be a source of comfort. In our mosque, as we read through sacred passages in the Qur'an, I often take notice of my fellow congregants. We are an unchanging cluster, as unchanging as the words on the pages in front of us. Our eyes are the same as the eyes of our great-grandparents, swooping up the same words from same holy texts. I imagine a similar feeling among the Copts when they pray from their Bible and maybe even the Jews with their Torah. As our congregants chant in unison, we are representations of the words. The words are representations of us. Our words, our voices, all become one. An endless, singular sheet of permanence.

It seems people from the West think we are all the same. We

have the tendency to get offended by this conclusion. We mock them for their simple brains. We forcefully claim that only if you squint through life will you see us as all the same. But here is where I get confused. If you actually magnify things, you see that we are all the same, just as they probably are all the same. How odd that it is an insult to say everyone from one country is the same but a compliment to say everyone in the world is the same. How impossible it is to be at the same time an individual and a member of a group.

According to the way some people are talking, you would think without cyberspace there would have been no revolution. It is as if the machines, themselves, are waging war on Mubarak. The machines are what organized the protests. The machines have a social conscience. The people are just instruments of the machines. I try to remain untainted by the flood of all this technology. After all, I don't have a computer, not such an unfortunate truth. I prefer to watch the pigeons bounce off each other inside their coop, a cluster of essentially identical creatures seeking an escape where there is none.

METRO

Justine Dymond

The year the Berlin Wall fell, I was living in Paris, sharing an apartment with two French students on the fourth floor of an old, rundown building. Despite the building's state, it had a concierge and an elevator, a rickety metal one with an accordion gate. I was living the bohemian dream.

Besides rent, one of my major expenses was transportation. I was taking classes at the various campuses of Université de Paris. The closest course, an art history course, was at Le Sorbonne, which was walkable, but the other campuses—Juisseau, the Grand Palais, and especially St. Denis and Nanterres—meant a Metro ride. For probably the equivalent of $20 per month, I could get a student pass, a laminated ID that had a little pocket for a new unlimited ride ticket every month. Occasionally, I tried to see how long I could go without renewing my ticket.

On buses, you could enter from the front or back and the bus driver didn't care whether you validated your ticket in the little machine or not. The Metro was a little harder because you had to go through turnstiles and, in some stations, you couldn't go under or over the turnstiles because they had sliding doors and there was no way to squeeze between them. If I was caught without my monthly ticket, I could be fined more than twice as much as the cost of the ticket itself, which you'd think would be incentive enough for me *not* to cheat. But I had expenses: food, wine, cigarettes, movies.

On both the Metro and the buses, you had to watch out for *contrôleurs*, the transportation police, and they were strict. One morning, as I made my way into the bowels of the subway station, turnstiles hissed open and banged shut, and trains rumbled underfoot. Commuters marched toward their destinations in silent, serious concentration. I slid my ticket through a turnstile, and the doors jerked open. There was shouting on the other side, but it sounded strange, as though underwater, bouncing off the tiled walls. I looked up to see a young, brown man chased by two *contrôleurs* with German shepherds. They caught him in an instant, slamming him against the tile walls. I had stopped halfway through the turnstile, gawking. Around me, the bang and hiss of other turnstiles continued, as did the uninterrupted march of commuters.

Such a scene would seem to be a cautionary tale. But the *contrôleurs* practiced racial profiling before it became a topic of controversy in the U.S. I could usually rely on their targeting young men who looked North African before their attention might turn to me. As a short, white girl I often slipped below their radar.

Unless they launched a take-no-prisoners strategy and fanned out across a Metro tunnel. Once, coming around a corner in a Metro tunnel, I was stopped short by a wall of *contrôleurs* who were checking everyone who came through. *C'etait chiant.* It was shitty. But there were no scary dogs, and I wasn't slammed against the wall. I was issued a fine.

In the spring of that year, an American friend of mine came to France and decided she wanted to stay a while. After a couple weeks of sharing my room, she found a *chambre de bonne*—a maid's room under the eaves, with a shared hallway bathroom—near Les Abbesses, a very trendy neighborhood.

The day Meema moved, the sky threatened rain. She filled her black trunk, with its sharp, neat lines, and we pushed and shoved and dragged it onto the rickety elevator. The metal cage was too small to fit both of us with the trunk, so Meema rode and I walked down the four flights of stairs.

At the lobby, we each took one end and carried the trunk

across the marble entrance, the concierge's face peering out from between lace curtains. The concierge was always spying on people in the lobby. We joked that maybe she thought Meema was an illegal, or worse, that there was a body in the trunk. As we left with our clunky package, the lace curtains twitched closed.

Despite having once been caught without a ticket, I still tried to get away with not updating my pass. Until Meema started her nanny job, she was on an even tighter budget. She would buy a packet of ten tickets, board a bus, and not validate her ticket. But she would stand near the stamping machine, in case *contrôleurs* appeared.

That day we boarded the rear of the bus, where there was space to rest the trunk on its side. I stood with my back to the door, facing Meema, both of us conscious of the stares boring holes into us. I never got used to how Parisians stared; it was shameless staring. In the U.S. people stare, but if you catch them at it, they look away as though they weren't watching you. Parisians always won the staring contest.

Just then Meema glanced over my shoulder and her eyes widened in surprise. I was about to turn my head when Meema hissed, "No, don't look. Contrôleurs."

I sucked in my breath. Neither of us had a proper ticket. At the same instant, the bus doors exhaled open. I turned and there they were, two groups of Metro police in black uniforms blocking the doors. No one could leave or board the bus. Except the *contrôleurs*, who now stormed on.

But we were in luck. At the back of the bus, a man panicked and jumped out of his seat. The *contrôleurs* rushed toward him, leaving the door cleared.

"Come on," I said, dragging the trunk. Meema quickly grasped my plan and we pushed and shoved the trunk off the bus. It fell to the ground, nicking one of its corners. Meema swore, but I ignored her and grabbed one end while Meema took the other. We lugged it around the block and down one street before we stopped, out of breath. My stomach was a tight ball with the fear that a *contrôleur* might run after us. But we were safe.

I looked for the nearest Metro entrance and updated my student pass.

When the Berlin Wall fell, I saw the events on a small, black and white TV in a friend's apartment. We watched for hours as East Germans and West Germans danced on top of the wall, sprayed champagne, and chiseled and hammered the wall into bits. A couple years later, I traveled to Berlin and picked up a souvenir piece of the wall, a chunk about the size of my fist. There's graffiti on one side and the rest is a gnarl of stone mixed into concrete. At the Checkpoint Charlie museum, there are photos and stories of the people who smuggled others across or tried to get over the wall into West Berlin. I wished I could have been that brave, but I knew that I couldn't have done it.

In the Metro that day when *contrôleurs* chased the young man with dogs, for a moment I froze, shocked out of my prosaic routine. The turnstile closed behind me with a hiss. The *contrôleurs* pulled the man out of the station. No one else seemed to notice, going about their business in the Metro, as though nothing had happened.

I didn't yell or protest. I didn't say a word. I joined the silence.

OUT THERE

Doug Bolling

The man in the 1920s smoking jacket
and argyle socks, a lean eyed
Victorian face, the trim moustache
& brows.

I fly often he says, my soul mate
for the journey.

Each flight a story waiting to be
told, a pinch of plot, a beginning
unless in medias res, whatever
it takes to unfold, grab the
juices awhile.

I look around he says.
Seventy, eighty fellow pilgrims
en route to hell or worse.

Each one has a story hidden
inside the covers, the little
navigators we call neurons.

Look around he says.
See how they show only
a mask, keep so much hidden
like scared rabbits blending
in as the dogs run by.

When they talk they don't.
Just a passing of words
to keep up the game,
fluff tossed off and
soon forgotten.

As for me I'm unclear
why I keep coming back
for more, twenty, thirty
flights a year just to
pretend I'm on a mission,
a real dude packed up and
ready, the diary full,
somebody out there in
wait mode wanting me
to land, begin the magic
all over again.

THE TROJAN HORSE

William Quincy Belle

Alexei finished doing a compile and uploaded the executable code to the test machine. He swiveled around in his chair and faced Ivan. "That's it, buddy. Over to you. I think I outdid myself this time. I've got things buried so deep, there is no damn way Symantec or McAfee will get it out, never mind detect it."

Ivan chuckled. "Okay, Mr. Smarty-pants, let me be the judge of that." He shook his finger at Alexei in a sign of admonishment. He swiveled in his chair to another console and tapped away at the keyboard.

"What's up, guys?" Dmitri strode into the room. He was the brains behind the outfit and always acted the part by wearing a suit. Even when Dmitri took off his suit jacket, he never took off his tie.

"I've uploaded the new version of the Trojan," said Alexei, looking at Dmitri. "If I do say so, this is going to be a good one."

Dmitri smiled. "Good stuff, Alexei." He turned to Ivan. "You'll put it through its paces?"

"I'm already on it," said Ivan without turning around.

"I snagged ourselves a new contract with a group operating out of Hong Kong. If we furnish them with email addresses and personal information for fifty thousand, they will pay us a good buck. If we give them a hundred thousand, they will give us all a nice bonus. And when we get more, the scale will go up. Let's hope this latest effort does the trick as we could be looking at a good profit."

Alexei had spent the past few months developing what he thought was the mother of all rootkits. Once this software was activated, it would overwrite the boot sector of a computer and put in its place a clever but nasty series of checks and balances which provided a renewable buffer between the operating system and the hard disk. Once it was in place, it would be virtually impossible to get it removed without wiping the entire hard drive clean and doing a fresh install. Alexei had inserted a number of load points into the operating system itself so, even if something put a fresh copy of the boot sector back, one of the other load points would kick in and restore the infected boot sector. If any of the anti-virus scanners kicked in, the Trojan would operate the disk interface so that any of the infected folders, the infected boot sector, or infected system files would be automatically replaced with a clean uninfected copy. Symantec or McAfee would keep reporting everything was okay because they could never gain access to the infection. The user would go about their day unaware their machine was compromised, their keystrokes were being recorded, and their personal information was being relayed back to Alexei's group through an untraceable worldwide anonymity network.

Dmitri and group had successfully deployed several such Trojans in the past two years. Anti-virus software eventually caught on to their work and they then had to modify things to further disguise their code, but any fresh deploy usually gave them several months to even a full year before a Trojan was rendered unusable. Despite the coverage in the newspapers of computer viruses and the importance of safety measures, the general level of security wasn't all that good. The average home computer owner had no clue what was going on. They bought a machine; they surfed the Net; they played games and shopped online, but they really had no idea how anything worked.

Dmitri stood behind Ivan and watched him work on the test machine. The three of them had developed a significant operation with a number of so-called products which netted them all a tidy profit. In addition to viruses and Trojans, they had assisted several pharmaceutical websites in emailing advertisements to millions of users to drum up sales, all with a commission. Business was good.

"Are you taking Dominika to that new movie tonight?" Dmitri hadn't stopped watching Ivan, but the question was directed to Alexei.

"Yeah, I plan to. I figured if I got out of here by five, we'd have enough time for dinner before the seven-thirty show." Alexei was lounging in his seat, watching Ivan work on the test machine.

"Sounds good," said Dmitri. He half turned to Alexei, but kept his eyes on the screen of the test computer.

There was a knock at the door. Ivan stopped typing. Dmitri turned and looked at Alexei. Alexei looked at Dmitri. All three of them had perplexed looks on their faces. Nobody knocked at their door. Ever. Nobody even knew they were there. Dmitri had rented the office space a few years back and had set up a dummy company name so no one would ever know about their operation.

"Who's that?" Alexei turned to the door.

"Beats me," said Dmitri. "Maybe it's the super."

Dmitri walked over to the door, which led into the corridor. He turned the knob and pulled the door open to find a man in a suit holding a piece of paper. "Yes? May I help you?" Dmitri said in Russian.

The man hesitated and said in English, "Are you Mr. Dmitri Ivanov?"

"Yes," said Dmitri in English.

"Are Mr. Ivan Lebedev and Mr. Alexei Pavlov here with you?"

Dmitri now looked perplexed. "Would you mind explaining what this is all about?"

"Not at all," said the man. He stepped to one side, turned to look up the hall and said, "Gentlemen," while gesturing to the open door.

The next few moments happened quickly, so quickly that Dmitri, Ivan, and Alexei didn't have any time to grasp what was going on. Six men rushed into the room from the hallway. They were all wearing latex gloves. The first two men stepped through the doorway, grabbed Dmitri's arms, picked him up, and carried him into the center of the room before forcibly seating him in a chair. The other four men paired off; two went to Ivan and two went to Alexei. Each man pulled out a roll of duct tape and fastened a forearm to the armrests of the two programmers' chairs.

Ivan and Dmitri were stunned into silence but Alexei yelled. "Hey! You can't do that!" One of the two men standing over Alexei slapped him hard. The blow stunned Alexei and he fell silent. The men taped the arms and the legs of Dmitri, Ivan, and Alexei to their chairs. They pulled out rubber balls and forced one into each of their mouths, then ran a band of tape around their heads to ensure they couldn't spit the balls out.

In the meantime, the seventh man had shut the door to the corridor, found an empty chair, and brought it around. He seated himself, unbuttoned his suit jacket, and crossed his legs. The other men grabbed the three chairs holding Dmitri, Ivan, and Alexei and lined them up to face him.

"Gentlemen, my name is Mr. Alan." He glanced at the paper he held in his latex-gloved hand. "Now if I have this correctly, you are Dmitri Ivanov." Mr. Alan pointed to Dmitri. "And you are Ivan Lebedev and you are Alexei Pavlov." Mr. Alan pointed to each man.

Mr. Alan folded the piece of paper and put it in an inside pocket in his suit coat. "I'm sure you are all curious who I am and why I am visiting, so we will dispense with the civilities and get right to the heart of the matter." He looked down and brushed a piece of lint off one pant leg of his suit.

"The three of you have been working together for about two years now, producing various pieces of software of a dubious nature. You are working on the fringes of the computer world, taking advantage of the security holes to be found in many systems and taking advantage of the general gullibility of a naive public. Far be it for me to stand in judgment of anyone conning a mark. Caveat emptor." Mr. Alan paused and looked at each of the three men. They stared back wide-eyed.

"However, you targeted my organization. We could argue that casting one's net on the Internet means we cast a wide net with little concern where that net falls. Such is the nature of the beast. But when one is attacked, when one is compromised, one feels the need to take remedial action to ensure they remain safe and secure."

Mr. Alan turned to Alexei. "Mr. Pavlov—Alexei—I believe you are the author of the Trojan horse called the May Blackhole." Mr. Alan waited a moment as if to give Alexei a chance to respond, but the ball gag prevented him from saying anything.

"This is an interesting bit of programming. Ingenious, in fact, the way it first exploits the ignorance of the user, then worms its way into the operating system and records keystrokes. From what I understand, and I understand little of these technical matters, it passes back to the host—that is, you—private and confidential information such as bank account numbers, PINs, passwords, etc. It's intriguing what you can find out about anybody if you are, so to speak, leaning over their shoulder and watching what they are doing at their computer. And with your key stroke recording, you are doing exactly that.

"Unfortunately, gentlemen, I can't allow you or anyone else to look over my shoulder. My operations are very important to me and very, very secret. Secrecy is the key to my success, in fact. Which brings me to why I am here." Mr. Alan put one hand up to his mouth and coughed. "Pardon." He smiled. "I wonder if I may be coming down with something. Either that or it's jet lag.

"You gentlemen have stolen information, secret information from my organization. I can't allow that to happen and I am here to take all the steps necessary to ensure that never happens again. I have had to spend a fair bit of time and resources—resources including money spent on consultants, anti-virus software, upgrading firewalls, etc.—to better protect myself and my colleagues from outside malicious attacks such as yours perpetrated against my computer systems."

All eyes were fixed on Mr. Alan; the eyes of his three captives and the eyes of his six cohorts. Mr. Alan was in command.

"Do you know what the total cost of spam is to the world? A recent report in the *Journal of Economic Perspectives* estimates the overall cost to be $20 billion. That takes into account lost productivity due to spam and the additional resources necessary to combat it. Twenty billion dollars! Gentlemen, that is a lot of money. Now, if you and your buddies were making $20 billion, well, heck, I would want a slice of that pie, but the fact is, what you make overall is a mere pittance compared to the cost to the world. The same report estimates the global profit to be only $200 million dollars. Imagine that for every dollar of profit you are causing one hundred times the damage. Sounds pretty inefficient to me.

"Of course, that is talking about spam. If we move into the area of Trojans, viruses and whatnot, we've moved into the area of corporate espionage and who knows what fortunes can be made there?

"Now my Russian friends here were of the mind to rid the world of your presence permanently. However, after careful reflection, I thought it would be better, if not best, to use your folly as an example to others who may be tempted to prey on the weak and stupid, but target the strong and smart." Mr. Alan smiled again. "You have to admit that you all being tied up right now is a display of strength, and the fact we're here should indicate we may be more than a pretty face." He paused. "Consider the fact we found you. I wonder why the American CIA or some other secret government service hasn't zeroed in on you." He shrugged. "I guess you must be too small of a fish to fry. Humph, many times we think we're safe at home in bed when, in reality it's a question of somebody bigger having not yet set their sights on us."

Mr. Alan looked at his cohorts. "Would you three start on removing the storage?" Immediately, three of the men began going around the room with screwdrivers, taking apart computer cases and removing hard drives. They disconnected laptops and took the entire machine. One man went into the next room.

Mr. Alan turned back to the trio of programmers. "Now, to best make an example of you, I need you to live. Therefore, nothing fatal will be done. Nevertheless, we must do something to dissuade the next group thinking of entering this dubious field of endeavor." Mr. Alan uncrossed his legs and re-crossed them the opposite way. "I thought the easiest thing to do would be to remove a digit."

One of the Russian thugs pulled out a pair of wire cutters. The three programmers recoiled at the sight of the tool. Alexei yelled and thrashed around in his chair. The chair teetered and fell onto one side. Another man pulled the chair upright.

Mr. Alan looked at this scene with utter detachment. "Are you familiar with Michael Moore?" He raised an eyebrow as he looked at each of them. "He's an American filmmaker who does excellent investigative documentaries. In his film *Sicko* about the American health care system, he talks with a gentleman who cut off the ends of two fingers with his table saw. Since he didn't have health insurance, he had to pay out of his own pocket to have the fingers re-attached. I'm not sure how the hospital came up with this pricing schedule, but they wanted $12,000 to re-attach the ring finger and $60,000 to re-attach the middle finger." Mr. Alan shook his head. "Imagine that the United States is the only advanced industrialized nation which does not offer its citizens universal health care. Shameful.

"In any case, I estimated that it cost my organization about two hundred thousand dollars to respond to the little security breach you caused. We had to change passwords, move accounts, reformat hard drives, hide transactions, etc. etc. It's amazing how such costs rack up, but technology isn't cheap and, if you want the best, you have to pay top dollar.

"So I decided, based on the cost of $60,000 per finger, that I would take the right middle finger of each of you for a grand total of $180,000. Not quite two hundred thousand, but what the heck, I'll eat the difference.

"As I said, I want to create a deterrent out of this, a warning to others. Therefore, we are going to film the amputations and post them online. We will include your names and contact information, so if anybody wants to verify the authenticity of the video clips, they can speak with you directly. Since you all speak English fluently, I'm sure it will be fairly easy for you to enlighten most of the international crowd.

"Shall we begin?"

A man pulled out a small video recording device and pointed it at Dmitri. Without warning, the man with the wire cutters came forward, grabbed a hold of Dmitri's right hand, moved the instrument into place, and snapped. Even though Dmitri had a ball gag still in place, his muffled yelling filled the room. Alexei cried and shook his chair around again. One of the thugs held it so it wouldn't tip over. Ivan remained silent. Mr. Alan glanced at Ivan and saw that he had wet himself.

The thug with the cutter moved to Alexei. Alexei let out a long muffled yell, then his head pitched forward onto his chest.

He had fainted. The thug snapped.

The thug then moved to Ivan. Ivan was perfectly quiet. He remained limp, passive. The thug amputated his finger and, yet, Ivan didn't react. Mr. Alan thought Ivan must be in shock.

"Bandage the wounds," said Mr. Alan. "We don't want anybody bleeding to death. These gentlemen are worth more to us alive than dead." The men set to work.

Three of the thugs came back into the room with a cardboard box filled with various items, including four laptop computers. Mr. Alan glanced at the contents. "Is that everything?" They nodded.

"Gentlemen, our work here is done. And I would think your work is done here, as well." The thugs removed the duct tape and freed the three programmers.

Mr. Alan looked at each programmer. "Dmitri, your wife is five months pregnant. You are going to be a father to a boy. A boy needs a father. Go back to studying law. I'm sure you will make a good lawyer. Alexei? Dominika is a fine girl. Treat her well. She would make a good life partner. Ivan. You've got good programming skills. There are many legitimate organizations who would like to have you. Seek them out."

All the men shuffled out the door. Mr. Alan followed, but paused at the door and looked back. "I trust we will never see one another again. I would hate to make a second visit because if I do, I guarantee I will follow the advice of my Russian friends and it will be the last visit."

Mr. Alan stepped out in the hall and closed the door. Within an hour, the videos were posted on YouTube. Within two hours, YouTube took them down but, by that time, people had copied the videos and posted them on various secondary video-sharing sites, along with the contact information of the three programmers. While the story spread somewhat, many thought the videos consisted of special effects. Only a few people called Dmitri, Ivan, and Alexei to confirm the story.

Six months later, Mr. Alan came back to Russia, but this time to visit a group calling themselves the Russian Freedom Fighters. This group of five rebel computer enthusiasts had hacked into secondary systems connected to Mr. Alan's organization. For this visit, Mr. Alan followed the guidance of his Russian friends and the Freedom Fighters ceased to exist. In a country of 150 million people and a record of questionable political stability, who's going to miss four men and a woman? Mr. Alan thought it was an unfortunate waste of talent, but had realized over the years that some people seemed detached from the results of their actions. They wanted something from somebody, and they didn't care if the other person suffered or not. They were determined to get what they wanted, regardless of the price paid by anybody else. Mr. Alan appreciated the idea was also applicable to him but, in this instance, he had the bigger stick. There is no honor among thieves, he reasoned. I don't care if you steal, just don't steal from me. Period. Mr. Alan also reasoned he was doing his share to stop these nefarious people from possibly bleeding the system dry. A wise parasite doesn't kill its host. That would be suicidal.

RIVER HIGH

Michael C. Keith

In the late spring, it rained hard and constant across central and south Missouri. When it stopped, the rivers, ponds, and lakes in the region had all risen to record heights. Flooding claimed fields, farms, animals, and businesses, prompting the governor to declare the entire area a disaster zone. A month later, I joined my two brothers-in-law, Terry and Alan, and we visited the Ozarks. Part of the trip included a planned canoe ride down the Gasconade River south of Rolla.

Living on the East Coast, we hadn't fully appreciated just how the monsoon-like weather had so impacted part of the "Show Me" state. We needed to be shown and would be. While we had heard about all the damage on the news, we figured that by the time we got there, things would be pretty much back to normal, and they were…pretty much.

When we rented our canoe at the Boiling Spring Campground, we were told to keep an eye out for the many trees and bushes that had been pulled from the banks into the river because of the long rains.

"Currents are real strong in places, too, 'cause of the rise, so watch yourselves, fellas," advised the gregarious rental clerk, as she led us to our canoe. "Be at Connor's Landing around four o'clock. Someone will be there to fetch you and the canoes and drive you back. This is the spot on the map right here. You should get there well before pickup 'cause of the conditions. Takes not much more than half the time now. Pretty much sit back and enjoy the ride, but keep clear of the floaters and floppers. They can mess up your day for certain."

"Floppers?" I asked.

"Yeah, the trees on the bank that have fallen into the river."

Terry had canoed the 280-mile river at different points back when he was an engineering student at the state university in Rolla, and he told us he'd capsized a couple times on it. He expected there was a good possibility we'd experience the same fate given the river's current state (*current* being the buzzword). His prediction didn't exactly instill calm in me, but I figured he might just be playing to my skittishness, since I'd never been canoeing before.

"Just make sure your Mae West is on snuggly, so if we flip over you won't lose it like I did once."

Before getting into the boat, I made sure my life preserver was on securely. I was a weak swimmer at best and figured it might be the only thing between me and drowning. Climbing into the canoe was a challenge in itself and we came close to taking a dunk before we had even set out. I took the seat in the stern and Terry claimed the one in the keel; this made us the helmsmen. Alan sat between us on the bottom of the canoe under its yoke. By the time we reached the middle of the river, I had a decent idea of what to do thanks to instruction from my fellow shipmates.

"Got it, guys. You're in good hands with Captain Keith," I assured them, as the canoe picked up speed on its own.

"Oh man, we're in deep trouble now," cracked Alan.

"We won't have to row much due to the strong currents. Just have to keep her from hitting anything. Looks like there's a bunch of debris on both sides," said Terry, surveying the river ahead.

The weather was perfect, but there were few people on the river. An hour passed uneventfully before things took a frightening turn…literally. Suddenly, the canoe swung left and we were headed toward a large fallen tree extending out from the shore. The swift current had us in its inescapable grip and, despite our frantic paddling, we crashed into the huge branches. I shouted to my brother-in-law to push away by shoving against an overhanging tree limb, but the current's fierce pull had its way with us.

The bow of the canoe dipped as the water rushed into it, and I ducked under one branch only to be struck by another. I just barely managed to cling to it as the canoe and my brothers-in-law vanished in the dense maze of leaning and broken tree parts and churning water. My inner voice screamed, "*Shit! Shit! Shit!*" as I gasped for air and clung to the branch, trying to gauge the distance to solid ground. *Maybe I can make it. Shimmy across*, I thought, my sense of doom opening full throttle. *I don't have the strength to lift myself up onto the limb. Damn! Okay, just drop into the water, then. You have a life jacket on. You'll just go with the current. Maybe meet up with Alan and Terry…if they're okay*, I told myself.

I attempted to take a deep breath, but couldn't because my lungs were constricted from my debilitating fear. Then I let go and dropped into the roiling river and was quickly pulled under and swept forward. In a matter of seconds, I found myself in shallow water no more than knee deep. *Thank God! I'm okay!* Still, with my strength sapped, it took everything I had just to stand.

"You all right?" shouted Alan, who was a few feet away, standing next to our submerged canoe.

Between us stood Terry, motionless. It took me a moment before I could catch my breath to answer.

"I think so," I grunted, and began to wade in his direction.

As I moved, I discovered that I was missing my watch and hat and had a large scrape on the upper part of my left arm.

"How about you guys?" I asked.

"Lost my camera and flip-flops," answered Terry, seemingly frozen in place.

"Something wrong? You hurt?"

"No…can't move too fast because the rocks under my feet are sharp as broken glass."

"You lose the paddle?" inquired Alan.

It was then that I realized I had. "Dammit, I guess so," I admitted, looking back to where I'd been hanging from the tree branch.

The three of us slowly waded to the bank while pulling and emptying out our sunken canoe.

"Told you guys this would happen," said Terry.

"Thanks for the heads up," I said, attempting to lighten the moment.

"Yeah, wish you'd told us before we planned on coming here," added Alan, with a smirk. "You'd make a lousy travel agent."

"Well, we got the canoe anyway," replied Terry. "We're lucky about that."

"But we lost a paddle, so how are we going to get down to the landing?"

"In circles," quipped Terry.

"I think I see it up the bank in some branches," announced Alan. "I'll get it."

A few minutes later, he returned with the lost paddle. Streams of blood trickled down his arms from the barbs he had encountered.

"Holy crap, man! What happened to you?" blurted Terry.

"Just scratches. Looks worse than it is," said Alan, handing me the retrieved paddle.

After catching our breath, we climbed back into the canoe and propelled to the middle of the river, vigilant for more dangers. Without further incident, we neared the pickup point about an hour later. When we spotted the mooring, we let out a collective sigh. Alan had managed to clean his bloody arms by dipping them into the moving river, and I noticed the bruise on my arm had already turned into a large blot of purple with skinny red tentacles reaching out from it in all directions.

We pulled the canoe from the water and dragged our weary bodies to a patch of shade and pretty much collapsed. No one said anything as we each contemplated the significance of what had happened to us. Finally, I broke the silence by commenting that I thought we were lucky to be alive.

"Nah, it wasn't as bad as when I flipped the canoe back when I was in college," said Terry.

"What do you mean?" I asked.

"I died," replied Terry, laughing at his own joke.

In the days and weeks that followed, our mishap became the stuff of legend. In our epic retelling, we had all died… many times.

RE: YOUR BROTHER

Frank Mundo

Were it up to me
my last image of you
wouldn't be
so far so close
to the maddening tree
pale-putrid, blind-beaten
rank and swollen
a pinata with all your candy stolen

Would I could
instead abstain
break fast and slow down
the Milk Queen's reign
I'd unattach, no
delete the strain
And disremember to remember you
smash-smushed, burned-bruised
rogue-river valley-coot
a strangely strange yet familiar fruit.

EVERYTHING THAT LIVES

Jim Plath

It was the early part of spring; the first few weeks where the world could just as easily slip back into winter as turn green and sprout flowers. A dry month had left the grass brown and brittle. In the east, sunrise spilled coral light onto clouds that glided over barren branches like broken fingers along the tree line.

Gene was tall and thickset. Dark hair spilled over his ears and down his narrow shoulders. If a beard was something a man trimmed and styled, Gene's face was what happened when a man just stopped shaving. When he moved, he had the look of sagebrush caught in a breeze.

Weekend sojourns in the deep woods were a habit for Gene. Having company was the novelty. A yard behind him, Aggie dragged her feet across the forest floor, scraping parched earth and snapping fallen twigs with every step. With wisps of blond hair leaking from under her red baseball cap, and a soft build beneath her thermal shirt, Aggie had the look of someone in a makeshift disguise.

Gene looked back to see Aggie falling farther behind. "Pick your feet up when you walk. You'll keep up easier."

Aggie paused and rubbed her calf muscle. "I'm tightening up. I could use a rest."

"Right now?"

Aggie looked up. "Are we in a hurry?"

"No," he answered. "I guess we can stop for a bit, if it means you quit dragging your feet and making a racket."

Aggie repositioned the straps of her backpack against her

shoulders. "I didn't think making noise was a bad idea. I read if they hear you coming, most predators will just move on ahead of you."

"I wasn't thinking about that. It just sort of spoils the peace and quiet. Besides, there are not a lot of apex predators in these woods."

Aggie switched to a quieter step. "Doesn't need to be a bear or a wolf to be dangerous, you know."

Gene laughed. "Okay, well if I see any pterodactyl-size sparrows, I'll holler."

"Joke if you want, but everything that lives, kills."

"See a lot of killer tulips?"

Aggie's eyes widened. "Plants use resources that other plants need to survive."

"Yeah, well you can stop trampling the ground. I don't think the grass has it out for you."

"It's been too dry. I think the grass is already dead.

"Try not to think so much. You'll never really get anything out of this if you don't relax."

The air kept a chill past sunrise and into late morning. The winds rose, but red-winged blackbirds still sang from swaying branches. Gene smiled as he passed through a thicket of birch trees and considered all he didn't see. No billboards or neon signs peeking through a clearing, no stretch of interstate to spoil the aesthetic of un-fouled wilderness.

Gene bypassed the birches, placed his backpack on the ground beside a dead shrub, and approached a heartier tree. He took hold of the thickest branch he could reach and tested his weight against it.

Aggie closed the distance between them. "What are you doing?"

"Climbing." Gene hoisted himself upward. "I want to get a better look." He slung his midsection over the branch, then his leg. Perched six feet from the ground, he searched for the next branch within reach, then scaled higher.

Aggie stepped back. "What are you looking for?"

Gene shifted his weight. "Nothing, really. I just want to see how far the view stretches."

"We should probably head back before too long. It's supposed to rain later."

Gene gripped the tree trunk and searched for his next move. "Look around you. We're not allergic to water, and the land needs it."

"Could be a bit of a storm though. The sky was pretty red earlier. Isn't there some kind of rhyme about that?"

Gene groaned as he reached for his next purchase. As he widened his stance, his foot fell on the curve of the branch beneath him. The tread of his sneaker lost its hold and Gene fell before he could scream.

Everything happened before Aggie could react. She saw the back of Gene's head as it struck the tree limb and snapped forward. His leg buckled under his body as he hit the drought-hardened turf to a sound like a bass drum. The fall forced the air from his lungs so that when Aggie reached his side, all she heard was short bursts of air squealing in his throat.

Aggie dropped to her knees and swung her backpack around her shoulder. From a front pocket, she drew her cell phone. It had no reception. "Dammit! Gene, can you hear me? Do you have your phone with you? We need to call for help."

Gene clutched the back of his head where dark, wet hair clung to his scalp. The leg that suffered the full force of his fall bent outward at an impossible angle. He parted his lips and whispered, "In the car."

"Can you move?"

Blood seeped through his jeans at the vertex of his leg's gruesome bend. A deep red stain grew like a gathering cloud. His face twisted around his eyes. "Hurts."

She couldn't carry him, and trying would only slow her

down. "Your leg is broken, and I'm sure you've got a concussion. I don't want to leave, but I don't think it's safe to move you."

"Go. Hurry."

Aggie left her bag beside Gene, rose to her feet, and sprinted back in the direction from which they came. She considered that it had taken them all morning to wander so deep into the woods, and wondered how long it would take her to run back. The undergrowth fanned her legs with each stride as her feet hurled dry dirt and detritus in her wake. Red-winged blackbirds launched themselves from the windswept limbs of birch trees in her path.

The air was milder on her skin, but too much of it, too fast, numbed her throat and burned her lungs. Her muscles tightened and ached, like hot water pooled beneath her skin. She held out her phone, hoping to find a signal faster, then, she could reach the car.

As Aggie's gait slowed, something struck her left leg. It was blunt, like a blow from a wooden plank, then sharp. She dropped her phone as she extended her arms ahead of herself, fell, and tumbled forward. She felt the twinge of broken skin as she lifted her leggings above her knee. Two thin streaks of blood dribbled down her shin.

Aggie searched the ground for movement, rustling grass blades, or some sign of the thing that had bitten her. She found nothing. A documentary once explained some snakes give warning bites which don't inject venom, but she had no way of knowing. Gene was well out of sight, as was the bike-path that would lead back to the car. Her cellphone had landed a few feet ahead of her. She crawled to it. It still showed no signal.

Aggie imagined Gene, far behind her, under waves of skeletal trees, so in need of time's swift passage. He needed her to run, find help, and tell someone where to find him. Running would increase her heart-rate and pump the venom faster through her blood stream. She needed to be slow and calm; he needed her to run and hope. Aggie rose to her feet, breathed deep, and put two fingers to the pulse in her neck, imagined it slower until it did slow.

She looked down at her feet, and checked her pulse again. It steadied. Aggie stepped forward, sliding her shoes past the splintered remains of fallen nests and woody debris. The soles of her shoes scraped dry earth with every measured step.

CRYSTAL CLEAR

Olga Wojtas

The shouting and gunfire was getting closer to the hotel. Martin pressed himself against the carpet as though he was trying to burrow through it. Lynne wriggled in the direction of the window.

"Stay down!" whispered Martin. "It's a bloodbath out there! They'll have snipers, grenades…"

Whispering, as though the mob might overhear him. Not for the first time, Lynne thought of Nick. Nick wouldn't be skulking away out of sight, despite his broken dreams. Had he tried to negotiate with the rebels? Had he realized there was no point, and decided to go down fighting?

"This is all your fault!" whispered Martin. "We should have gone to Scarborough."

They might be about to be executed in the middle of a foreign revolution, thought Lynne, but at least they hadn't gone to bloody Scarborough. At least she had had some excitement before she died.

———— ✦ ————

It was the sapphire-blue bottle that first caught her eye in the supermarket, with its distinctive black K.

Then the special introductory price for Kristalskaya Vodka, whose smooth taste was thanks to the clear crystal waters from Volkistan's towering Zakladka mountains.

Then the competition to win a luxury holiday for two in Volkistan with a twelve-word slogan for Kristalskaya Vodka.

She had never heard of Volkistan but it had to be better than

Scarborough. And a luxury holiday for two had to be better than a B&B with Martin and Martin's sister and brother-in-law and their three screaming kids.

Lynne had never had any luck in any competition but this time, she won.

Martin was appalled by the prospect of visiting a former Soviet republic, no matter how good its vodka was, and complained all the way there. As they came in to land at its international airport, he said: "It's a shed in a field!"

He had a point, but he wasn't taking in the bigger picture: quaint wooden houses and shining onion-top domes in glorious meadowland surrounded by spectacular peaks, the Zakladka mountains themselves.

The plane touched down and the flight attendant approached them. "Mr., Mrs., Watkins? Please to leave first."

They emerged from the plane to find a red carpet at the foot of the steps, with a welcoming committee, press and television reporters, and a brass band. The band struck up a jaunty tune as Lynne and Martin descended. A tall, broad-shouldered man came to greet them, slightly overweight, his dark hair slightly too long, but it suited him, Lynne thought.

"Mr., Mrs., Watkins, welcome to Volkistan!" he said, one of his teeth flashing gold. "We are honored to have such distinguished guests. I am minister for tourism, Nikolai Yakovlevitch Akhmanov. Please to call me Nick."

A young woman with long fair plaits, wearing traditional costume, came forward, carrying a tray with a Kristalskaya bottle and three glasses. Nick poured out the vodka and handed out the glasses. The camera crew crowded forward.

"Mrs. Watkins, congratulations on your award-winning slogan. Please to tell it to us."

Lynne raised her glass to the battery of cameras. "It's crystal clear that Kristalskaya puts you on top of the world," she said.

Everyone applauded. Nick drained his glass and smashed it

on the ground. Lynne drained her glass and smashed it on the ground. Martin took a sip, grimaced, and put his glass back on the tray.

And then they were in a roomy limousine, heading for Volkistan's capital, Volkograd, Lynne sitting between Martin and Nick. She exclaimed in delight at everything they passed: the mountain waterfalls; the white storks feeding in a field; a multi-colored, multi-domed edifice which turned out to be the Sepulchre of St. Vasily, the Double-Jointed.

"Your country is so beautiful," she said.

"This makes my heart very happy," said Nick, his tooth flashing. "I have many ideas as minister for tourism. I have MBA from Laramie University, Wyoming. My dream is for Volkistan to be in top ten of world destinations."

Martin snorted and Lynne jabbed her elbow in his ribs. She admired a man with the capacity to dream.

When they reached Volkograd, Nick apologized for the grim concrete blocks of flats. "Symbol of unfortunate past," he said. "Now we go to modern building, Volkistan's first five-star hotel. And you, Mr., Mrs., Watkins, are first guests!"

The staff were lined up outside waiting for them and applauded as they got out of the limousine.

"Bloody hell," muttered Martin, "this was supposed to be a free break—what if they all want tipping?"

Lynne managed to kick his ankle.

Nick escorted them into the palatial reception area. "You are tired after long journey from UK. You have small dinner with specialities of region, you sleep, tomorrow holiday starts!"

He grabbed Martin in a hug and kissed him on both cheeks. Then he shook hands with Lynne who felt rather snubbed.

The small dinner turned out to be seven courses accompanied by a bottle of Kristalskaya and a string quartet.

"What is this?" Martin kept asking as each course arrived, and the waitresses would beam proudly and say: "Is specialty of region." Lynne thought it all tasted wonderful.

The next morning, they came down for breakfast, Martin complaining about indigestion, which Lynne suspected was a hangover. But the dining room was deserted.

A teenage girl appeared. "Mr., Mrs., Watkins? Most sorry for inconvenience. No staff today. Today is revolution."

"What?" said Martin.

"Revolution," she repeated. She mimed firing a machine gun and then mimed getting shot. "Today please to stay in room. Tomorrow everything good, trip to Land of a Hundred Lakes, very nice."

"Now look here—" said Martin.

There was the sound of distant gunfire.

"Please to hurry to room," said the girl, handing them a plastic bag and disappearing out of the front door.

In their room, they found the bag contained food and drink, but Martin said he felt sick. He refused to get off the floor, and by the time the rioting reached the hotel, he was curled in the fetal position, sobbing.

There was a knock on their door. "Mr., Mrs., Watkins?" A young man's voice.

"Don't let them know we're here!" wailed Martin.

"Please to repeat?" said the voice.

Lynne opened the door and a soldier came in.

"Mr., Mrs., Watkins, you are ghosts," he said.

Martin flung his arms round the soldier's boots. "Don't kill me! I'm begging you, don't kill me!"

Shouldn't that be don't kill us? thought Lynne.

"No kill!" said the soldier, looking perplexed. "You are ghosts. New president invites you to dinner."

"Please tell the new president," said Lynne, "that we are very honored to be his guests."

❖

A limousine whisked them to the presidential palace. Perhaps Nick was still alive, thought Lynne. Perhaps the former ministers had only been imprisoned. And she could use this evening to plead for him, to explain that he had ideas for the country's future...

They walked into the state banqueting hall, which was packed with dignitaries.

"Mr., Mrs., Watkins! It is pleasure to see you again! Please to take seat beside me."

Nick, wearing a scarlet presidential sash across his dinner jacket, was at the head of the table.

After the national anthem had been sung and they were eating gherkin soup with carp dumplings, Lynne asked if many people had died in the revolution.

"No, thanks goodness, everyone is very well apart from boy who fell off skateboard and broke arm."

"But—all the shooting—"

"We shoot in air to celebrate, we do not shoot one another! We are Volkistani, all brothers!"

"What about the former president?"

Nick shrugged. "My older brother. No good. No MBA from Laramie University, Wyoming. I tell him, go home to farm, look after pigs, I look after country. He is little bit mad with me right now, but will be okay."

All round the room, people were shouting something and downing glasses of Kristalskaya.

"What are they saying?" asked Lynne.

"Traditional toast, *pod stolom*," said Nick.

"What does that mean?"

"Under the table," said Nick.

Lynne downed a glass of Kristalskaya in one. "*Pod stolom*," she said.

"Very fine," said Nick. "And tomorrow, we go to Land of a Hundred Lakes."

"What, you too?" said Lynne. "Don't you have to run the country?"

Nick called to a man in military uniform who laughed and replied.

"Colonel says he will keep eye on things until I get back."

Lynne was feeling warm. Her thigh was feeling particularly warm, because under the table, someone was stroking it.

She downed another Kristalskaya. "*Pod stolom*," she said. She was feeling on top of the world.

REAL MICKEY

Nancy Scott Hanway

My son is only three, but he understands that stories are make-believe. "Oh, Mama," Griffin says if I pretend that magic is real, "that's just in fiction!" As we're saying prayers before bed, he asks me if God is just a character in our family Bible. I've been aware for a long time that he's exceptionally bright. On his first birthday he had a one-hundred-word vocabulary. Now—because his babysitter explained to him that English comes from other languages—he sometimes insists that I get out the etymological dictionary to check on the origin of a new word. It's a little creepy.

The older he gets, the more I'm frightened of his intelligence. Early on, it was because a pediatrician warned us that it could be a sign of autism. Now, it's because I worry that someday he won't need me. He's still in that delicious preschool stage, bursting with love. He crawls onto my lap in the morning, wraps his hands around my neck, and kisses me tenderly. He learned to write his letters in Montessori preschool, and he scrawls "I LOVE MAMA" on dozens of scraps of paper that he stuffs into my shoes.

"Why are you so worried?" his dad asks. "He's still a little kid. Look at his Mickey fixation."

Because, despite his big brain and early nihilism, my son worships Disney cartoons. As a testament to the all-consuming power of the Disney Corporation, Griffin believes wholeheartedly and passionately in Mickey, his favorite character. And he has no interest in going anywhere on any continent that doesn't somehow involve The Mouse.

When I tell him that we're traveling to Paris after Christmas, he sticks out his lower lip. "I don't want to go."

"It's fun, sweetheart. You'll love it."

"Nope. Stupid Bear-is."

"Paris," I correct him. "Mama once lived there."

"Nope," he says as if it's final. "Nope, nope. No Bear-is Paris."

"There's a Disneyland there." And this is where I get a terrible idea. It doesn't seem like such a bad idea at the time. After all, his dad and I have already decided to take him to Euro Disney. "Mickey has a house there."

"Mickey's house?" His eyes light up. He's adorable, with blond hair, enormous blue eyes, and dimples. A colleague once told me that Griffin looked like Christopher Robin. I made the mistake of repeating this to Griffin, and we had to process this comment—that he looked like a fictional character—for days.

"Yes," I say, encouraged. "When Mickey's in Paris, he lives at the Disneyland there."

We look it up on the map. He frowns, tracing the dot I have told him is Saint Paul, Minnesota, to the one that is Paris. "Which one is Mickey's house?"

"That's Paris right there."

"Mama," he says. "Mickey's house will be on the map."

From the minute we arrive in Paris, where we are spending five days, Griffin begins talking about visiting Mickey's house. While eating chocolate crepes on the Champs Elysées, sitting on a tourist boat on the Seine, riding on a nineteenth-century carousel, strolling through a zoo. No matter how many child-friendly tourist spots we hit, he keeps asking, "So, where's Mickey's house?" And he quotes the brochure we got in the mail: "We're talking about just one place—Disneyland Paris! A place where the whole family will have the time of their lives!"

"There are other things to see," his dad says.

"I saw the Eiffel Tower," Griffin says. "There's nothing else for me here."

We arrive at Disneyland Paris practically at dawn on a gray, chilly day. Icy rain spits on us as we stand in line for tickets. The very first thing we do once we enter the gates is wait in another line so Griffin can meet Mickey. Even though he questions the existence of God, he sees nothing odd in seven-foot, plush cartoon animals walking around and hugging children. He is vibrating with excitement, jumping up and down and shrieking, "Mickey, Mickey!"

The other kids seem frightened or awkward around Mickey. They cry when he hugs them, or they refuse to sit on his lap for a picture.

When it's his turn, Griffin runs up to Mickey and gives him a huge hug. "Mickey, I've been waiting to see you!" A collective "aaaawwww" goes through the line. Some of the parents nudge their kids, saying in English or French, "See, that boy isn't scared."

As we leave the line, Griffin says, "Now I want to see Mickey's house."

"Did you ask Mickey where it is?" I say, smiling.

Griffin shrugs. "He wouldn't tell."

And this is where we discover the problem. I didn't actually check on whether Mickey had a house at Euro Disney before we arrived. There's one in Florida at Disney World. I assumed there would be one in here. Come on: Cinderella has a castle, Mickey has a house. But there's no lodging for Mickey in Paris. And Griffin can already make out letters. He knows that Mickey starts with "M." We can't lie and pretend that some little faux cottage is Mickey's house. And besides, in Mickey's place, there would be pictures of Mickey and Minnie. Griffin keeps repeating this. "Mickey and Minnie *share* a house."

All day he is relentless in his search, even tugging on one of the guards' coats to ask directions. We tell him that I was wrong, that Mickey doesn't live in France, he just visits. We tell him that Mickey's house is in Florida, where we will go someday.

"No," he screams. "Madeline has a house in Paris! Mickey has one too!"

"Madeline's fiction," I say, feeling ridiculous.

"I know," he says, sobbing. "But it's about a real person!"

"Mickey's a story too."

"You're lying!" he wails. "I just met him!"

He collapses, dispirited and crying, beside Cinderella's castle after we tell him, in desperation, that when Mickey is in Paris, he rents a room from Cinderella and her prince.

He looks us at with disdain, tears rolling down his cheeks. "That's stupid. Mickey doesn't live with humans. He's a *mouse*!"

We take him for the third gelato of the day. He has refused real food and has eaten nothing but chocolate gelato since 5 a.m., when he had a stale croissant. And we finally realize that it's a lost cause to convince a jet-lagged, sugar-buzzed three-year-old that Mickey doesn't live here anymore. We drag him, kicking and shrieking, out of Disneyland and onto the train back to the city. French families edge away from us, looking at our red-faced beast in horror.

He is still crying a little the next morning when we tell him that we are visiting a king's house.

"Palace," he says, hiccupping. "That's what a king's house is called."

"Its name is Versailles."

"Oh." He sits up. "I know about that." It turns out that his babysitter—the preternaturally smart daughter of a colleague—played the storming of the Bastille with him before we left Minnesota.

And because his babysitter told him the story, he transfers all of his passion for Mickey's house to Versailles. On the way he asks a thousand questions about the king who was killed. Was he a real person or a storybook king? Where did he go to the bathroom? Could he eat whatever he wanted?

As we wander the grounds, he asks, "So why did they cut

off his head?"

I explain, as well as I can, about the extreme poverty of the peasants and the obscene wealth of the royalty. He cocks his head to one side. "They killed him because he wouldn't share?"

"More or less," I say, and he nods approvingly.

"What is this?" his dad asks. "The Richard Scarry version of French history?"

"You try," I say, and his dad launches into a long explanation. He gets as far as telling Griffin about "Let them eat cake!" when our son puts a hand on his dad's arm as if he is dealing with a particularly long-winded old person. "Mama explained about the sharing thing."

The next day, in the Louvre, we see a huge painting of Napoleon being crowned, and Griff asks if he was a good man or a bad one.

"He wanted the whole world for himself. So I guess you could say he was a very selfish man."

"Just like that other king!" Griffin pauses. "Did they chop off his head?"

"No, darling. They poisoned him."

He nods happily. "I love you, Mama." And I can tell that the balance of power has shifted. All is right with the world. I give a huge sigh of relief.

As we're boarding the train back to Paris, he asks, "Who's the king now?"

"Oh, they got rid of kings. Now they have a president. We passed by his office today."

Griffin leans against me and I can feel his languor, the heavy stillness of a child about to fall asleep. He gives a big yawn. "Mama, that president."

"Yes, sweetheart?" I stroke his hair, wondering what he will ask. I assume he'll ask if the president likes croissants or whether he gets to put people he doesn't like in jail. I relax against the seat, worn after a day of sightseeing and answering questions. But I'm happy.

"Let's ask him if he knows where Mickey lives."

———■◆■———

The next day we head straight for a tourist information office. I'm kicking myself for not thinking of this earlier. As we wait in line, Griffin stares obsessively at the slender man in a blue blazer who sits below a sign that reads "Information" in several languages.

"Does he speak English?"

"I don't know," I say. "We'll find out."

When we get to the front of the line, I launch into a long explanation about our predicament in my used-to-be fluent French, making sure I say the word "Mickey" several times for Griffin's benefit. The man frowns slightly. For a terrible moment I think he's going to refuse. Then he adjusts his glasses, looks down at my son, and says in English, "Mickey once lived in Paris. Now he is moved. Back to America."

"Moved?" Griffin asks. "Why?"

The man shrugs, lifting his eyebrows at the same time. "Mickey does not like it in Paris. He says it's too cold. So he comes for a few days, and then he returns to California."

Griffin considers this for a moment. "That's stupid. I like Paris. I like crepes."

The man smiles. "Would you like to take a tour of a chocolate shop?"

For the rest of our time in Paris, Griffin doesn't even mention Mickey. On the way back to Minnesota, I have to rescue his collection of Mickey and Minnie figurines, which he drops in airport bathrooms, leaves in waiting rooms, and abandons in seat pockets on each plane. I know that this sudden drop of interest in Mickey is perfectly normal. I know that all children switch from one childhood obsession to another, sometimes going through several in the same week. But I can't bear my son's abandonment of Mickey, whom he once held so dear.

INSIDE THE GREAT BARTENDER

Colin Dodds

It was his sky,
double you and his key,
the reply to why? was sky
and whiskey exploded in air
so nature could destroy her rogue sons.

The bartender was like the empty space
thieves leave
when they take a piece of furniture.

The Wily Hermit asked The Worst Man on Earth
what he dreams and The Worst Man on Earth
said he dreams he's invited to a ladies' parlor to sing arias
and arrives unshaven, stinking, caked with vomit.

The ladies tell him to go brush his teeth.
He pulls a tube of toothpaste from his pocket
and semen spills out of it, onto the rug.
"Jesus" they say "You can't even keep
your semen out of our carpet. Go help in the kitchen."

The Wily Hermit said he had his key—
whiskey and ginger ale
and that The Worst Man on Earth should stop by.

We're all inside of that great bartender tonight,
blinded by those clean patches of carpet

where you're almost certain something used to be.
Sobriety and wakefulness are not your friends
when they treat you like *that*.

The ephemera of the town
won't save anyone from the perils of friendship.
The Worst Man on Earth found a way to cheat the jukebox
but not the horrible evening.

And nothing ever wins for very long
but you pick a side all the same,
and root for whatever decomposes you the fastest.
Nature must destroy her rogue sons.

ROAD KILL

Liz Dolan

When my friend Sam calls and asks about my trip to Martha's Vineyard, I say, "I leave tomorrow."

"I'm off to Providence tomorrow," he says. "Come with me, would love the company. I'll drop you at the ferry."

"But I already have my bus ticket."

"Maybe they'll refund it. Be here no later than eleven."

At eleven the next morning, I am sitting on a chair in Sam's dining room amid cardboard boxes and stacks of business papers strewn on the table. At least I think it's the dining room. Because the trail of boxes and papers continue into the living room, it is hard to assign any purpose to any room other than storage. Silver platters, pitchers, ewers, spoons and teapots sit in corners, on shelves, under tables and chairs.

"Are you moving?" I ask. Sam purchased this apartment in Philadelphia ten years ago. Suddenly, I recall my husband telling me he had been in many apartments Sam owned in New York; they all looked as though he had just moved in or was just moving out. Sam still has his New York apartment and the house he purchased in Providence last year, plenty of storage space.

Sam, who has written books on early American silver and is a professor in the Decorative Arts Department of a prestigious university, takes out a long stemmed piece of colonial flatware from a newly opened Fed Ex box. "I can make a few hundred bucks a day buying and selling on eBay," he says. "By the way, we have to stop off for a quick lunch with friends of mine at one o'clock."

By noon, we have made our fourth trip up and down on the elevator carrying boxes, shopping bags, and duffle bags, which we stuff into Sam's Toyota. Thank God for the elevator, as he lives on the eleventh floor.

"I have to run to the post office," he says, and dashes out the door. I am beginning to wonder about the bus I could have taken.

When he returns, he says, "I have to empty the dishwasher." Then, "Oh, I forgot my diabetes shot." He sits down at the cluttered table, pushes the papers out of his way, pulls up the front of his shirt, pulls out the syringe, and injects himself, never skipping a syllable. He has not stopped talking since I arrived, as if someone was filming us and he's the voiceover. For all I know, he's shooting up some drug that makes him totally manic. I look away.

"Can I tell you a story? Wait, I have to drink something." He guzzles from a container of orange juice. "When I first bought this place, I went to the co-op board and asked to see the books. You'd have thought I'd asked them to pay my mortgage. The seventy-year-old president's white hair stood on end as if she'd stuck her finger in a socket. The treasurer screamed in my face and called me a troublemaker. I didn't give up until I saw those books. Transparency is one of the first rules of a co-op as you know, Liz."

Sam and my husband, Neil, renovated a tenement on the Lower East Side in the eighties when the neighborhood was a den of drug addicts and abandoned buildings. I always looked forward to meetings with Sam because he always spoke both intelligently and sparingly about the business of renovation. He had renovated a few other buildings prior to this one. I always respected his pragmatic approach to any and all difficulties that arose. His know-how saved us many headaches and also saved us huge sums of money.

"Recently, after many years away from the sacraments,"

Sam continued, "I went to confession to a black priest who is considered a seer by some of his parishioners."

While he reviewed the Commandments with me, he asked, "Do you covet your neighbors' goods?"

"No," I said, "I share both my goods and my talents." I told him about the shrew of a woman in the co-op who was trying to destroy my reputation.

"He said, 'You won't have to worry about her for long.'

She died three months later.

"Isn't that scary, Liz?" Sam probably talked the poor old woman to death. "Okay," Sam says, stretching up to his six foot four inches. "I think we're ready."

It's one o'clock. "Oh, one last thing," he says as he grabs a folder filled with checks and legal forms, which fall all over the floor. Sam and I crawl on the floor, picking up the scattered documents.

On the tiny elevator where a mousey-haired woman is waiting, I skulk in the corner carrying more packages as Sam holds the door open with his long leg and chats with a neighbor in the hall. She asks for what he owes her. Monies exchange hands, half of which she drops. One leg in the door, the other out, Sam bends over to help her pick up the money. I smile at the waiting woman.

"I know you," Sam says to her as he places both legs on the elevator. "You're Gene's sister; he is so nice. And if Gene is nice, you knooow what that means? You're nice, too. This is Liz; she's a famous writer." The woman stares at him.

"One last thing," Sam says when we get to the garage, "I have to take this jacket to the cleaners." On the back of the jacket are three Looney Tunes characters: Bugs Bunny, Porky Pig, and Elmer Fudd. "I bought it at a flea market. Gotta be worth five hundred bucks on eBay," he says. At the cleaners, Sam uses his two words of Vietnamese to ingratiate the clerk to get the twenty percent discount.

"No discount," she says. "Fifty dollar. Leather, have to send out."

"Sam," I say, "You should wear that jacket all the time."

Since it is long after one, I'm wondering how far away this luncheon is. When we arrive somewhere in suburban Pennsylvania close to two, "You are late," his friend says in a thick Russian accent.

Sam responds with his two words of Russian, "Rostrovia, Comrade." According to Sam, his Russian friend is going through a bitter divorce. His new girl has prepared a scrumptious lunch including shrimp salad, fresh mozzarella, and a fine merlot. Sam introduces me, "Liz is a famous writer."

Sam continues to talk nonstop. I am ecstatic these two people are here to absorb some of the shock. The Russian shows Sam an exquisite Japanese miniature. "The finest detail I've ever seen," he says. Then he shows Sam a filigreed silver spoon once owned by the King of Belgium. Then he places a two-foot high embossed, bronze trophy with wings jutting from its sides on the table. With his two words of German, Sam figures out from the inscription that it is a trophy given to an Austrian pilot in 1933.

"At least 35," Sam says. "At least 35,000." I am astonished.

"Where did you find it?" I ask. Nobody answers me. At any moment I expect 007 to kick in the door.

"Get a second estimate; it may be more." Monies change hands as we hug the delightful Russians goodbye. I ask them if they'd like to come with us. All three stare at me.

I left my home in Delaware at 8 a.m. Now it is 4 p.m. and I still have a six-hour trip ahead of me. Had I taken the bus, I'd already be in Martha's Vineyard. I could have roller-skated faster.

Revved up even more by lunch and Merlot, Sam continues talking. I am so tired I say nothing. "You're so quiet, Liz." I wish I were the kind of person who could drop off to sleep easily. Of course I could pretend. Now he is bragging about his three siblings. "We have thirteen college degrees among us; they are all multi-millionaires. Can I tell you a story, Liz?" *Sure, why not, what the hell, feel free.* I feel as though I'm trapped in a closet with Woody Allen pouring his New York angst all over me.

"My mother got my genius brother admitted to the Regents scholarship exam even though his principal said he wasn't eligible because his grades were not up to snuff. She called the Board of Regents. Imagine that in the late 50s. They said anyone could take the test. She went to the principal, listened to his spiel, then accused him of lying. My mother never took no for an answer. When she wanted something, she'd scream until she got it. After she got what she wanted, she'd be perfectly calm. 'Sometimes people won't help you because they're lazy,' she'd say, 'so you have to make them hop to it.' My father was very quiet," Sam adds. Gee, what a surprise.

"Thank God somebody was," I say. I suddenly realize I should be grateful that Sam is not a screamer. I wondered if screaming might get me what I needed right now but I hadn't the energy even to whimper.

"Because I was fragile from chest reconstruction surgery," he continues, "My mother didn't let me out much in those Syracuse winters. Probably why I got diabetes at 19, lack of Vitamin D." I wanted to say I never knew you were diabetic until today but I knew he'd conjure up the history of diabetes in the known world. "May I tell you a story?" he asks. We are only two hours into the trip. No traffic delays so far, thank Jehovah and Allah. "When I called Neil to borrow the money to cover the foreclosure on the house in Providence, do you know he said yes immediately? No questions asked; he even got a bank check to speed up the process for me."

"He trusts and respects you, Sam." At least he did until I tell him about this trip.

"Before I asked your husband, I asked my nephew, an international lawyer. He said he had no cash and his sister, a Johns Hopkins surgeon, also refused. I provided for them in my will but I am changing it as soon as I close this deal."

Twilight is descending. We are someplace in New Jersey. "How'd you like to hear some tapes Bernardo made for me?" Bernardo, Sam's partner, hails from Mexico and is an airline pilot. I'm thinking he became one after he met Sam to save his sanity. Who could live with Sam on a full time basis? He slips in the CD. Uber romantic guitar music accompanying four-part singing fills the air of the Toyota as I rest my head on the headrest. "Isn't it lovely and tranquil?" Sam asks. John Phillip Sousa would be lovely and tranquil right now as long as it drowned out Sam's nonstop chatter.

Unfortunately, he begins translating the words, "My love is the bird of youth, the life in my soul. My love is the sun, the moon, the stars."

"I know Spanish," I say. "But even if I didn't, I don't have to understand the words to enjoy the music, Sam."

"Your face is a sunflower, your eyes are like marigolds." Blah, blah, blah.

Then he begins to sing, "Mi amor volvera." Finally at 8 p.m. we arrive in Providence. "Watch for the ferry signs," he says. I can't wait to get there. We pull in to the ferry station, which has a huge closed sign hanging on its door. Oh my God, the ferry stopped running at the end of September, which means I am still two hours away from the ferry that is still running. I realize now I am being punished for every unkind word I ever vollied at my pain in the ass kid brother. "No problemo," Sam says. "You can stay over at the house."

Sam tells me he purchased this house after his friend hanged himself. I dare not ask where or why he hanged himself lest we be up 'til midnight. Besides, if he was Sam's close friend, I fully understand why he hanged himself. Sam bought it for

$159,000 a year ago. Now he hopes to sell it for $259.

We pull up to a huge Victorian with a wrap around porch on a dark, deserted street. We unload Sam's Toyota. I drag my suitcase up narrow steps to a huge bedroom with a bed and a lamp on a plastic Parson's table. In the dining room, there is a mahogany table and one chair. All the furniture has been auctioned. Obviously, because it is on the market, Sam has controlled his need to fill every nook and cranny with clutter.

"I'll sleep downstairs on the blow up," Sam says. "Let's go for Chinese." This trip has been a truly international experience. I don't need food; I need quiet, but no way in hell am I staying in this Bates mansion alone. "First I have to take my insulin," he says. Once again, Sam pulls up the front of his shirt and shoots up. I look away and wish I hadn't answered that fucking phone yesterday.

At the restaurant, Sam greets the waitresses, the cooks, and the tattooed patrons, "Nihao, ling ling." We sit under a neon light at a small wooden table with a wobbly leg. "Did you get a job yet?" he asks the sleek-haired waitress. "She's an architect," he says. "Liz is a famous writer." Over lo mein and garlic eggplant with plain white sauce, he says between mouthfuls, "When I return the money to Neil, I am bringing it directly to him to place it in his hand. I'll stay over."

Please no, I think. "That's a long trip," I say.

"No, no, I am so grateful to him." I'm already planning on not being home when Sam arrives.

At 8 a.m., Sam is yelling up the stairs, "Are you coming to the flea market? Bring your luggage. I'll drop you at the ferry."

"Sam, I'm sure there's a bus to the ferry, I don't want to be a bother," I yell back. I pray to the sweet Lord there's a bus to the ferry, to anywhere. For an hour and a half, Sam cruises through the flea market, skimming over silver or other articles of possible value, talking to everyone as though they are family. He reminds me of Elwood P. Dowd, the beneficent drunk in

Harvey, whose mother always said, "If you can't be smart, be nice."

"I've tried smart; nice works better," Elwood advised.

As we approach the bus station to which a dealer directed us, Sam repeats that if there is no bus, he'd drive me to the ferry. Even though I still have two hours on a bus and another hour on the ferry, then another hour on another bus, I would sooner ride in a rickshaw even if I had to pull it myself rather than spend two more hours with Sam who is just trying to be nice, God damn it.

If I ever get to Martha's Vineyard, I am supposed to meet friends there; I'm thinking of not contacting them and spending two weeks in total isolation. At the waiting area where I am reveling in the quiet, a young woman sitting on the bench next to me picks up my hat from the ground and says, "Hi, I think we're taking the same bus." I grab the hat from her hand without making eye contact and don't even say thank you.

SECOND OPINION

Scott Solomon

"There is something wrong with him," said Mom. "I just know it."

"Now, Mother, we've been over this before."

Dr. Lemuel Wise, my pediatrician, maintained a mostly loyal following.

"Franklin is fourteen years old, and he hasn't grown to 90% of his full height."

Mom's Wonder Bread, as of the summer of 1970, had yet to rise to the occasion.

"These things take time," noted the physician with fluffy white hair and a beard to match.

"All you doctors say the same thing," said Mom.

"Most of us need to be reminded rather than informed," said Dr. Wise.

In the bookless bookshelf behind Dr. Wise's desk, a floppy red hat with white trim and a pom-pom did its best, despite the season, to ho-ho-ho me through my Mom-mandated coat and tie.

"Don't remind me," said Mom in her tie-dyed T-shirt and bell-bottoms, pushing forty. "When Franklin was a baby, his testicles refused to descend. My husband and I looked for them in the bathtub every evening."

"I'll bet the family jewels showed up when least expected," said Dr. Wise with a wink that hoisted a small smile in my heart.

"That's beside the point. How is Franklin supposed to make it in high school this fall? He was so difficult to toilet train."

Dr. Wise stroked his beard to the tune of Mom squirming in her seat. "What say you, Frank?"

"But—"

"Mother, give him a chance."

"W-well." I almost forgot how to talk. "I'm well past toilet training."

"We're—I mean he's an excellent student, Dr. Wise."

"I know."

"We need to be certain he can continue to perform."

With a nod of his fluff, Dr. Wise plucked my grades out of a manila folder.

"That doesn't look like much," said Mom as she leaned forward in her chair and squinted.

"One mustn't be quick to judge," said Dr. Wise, wielding a pencil and connecting the dots. "Frank's height and weight plot out perfectly on a gradual upward incline."

"Define gradual upward incline."

"Slow and steady wins the race. Frank is a slow grower, but a grower just the same."

"How slow is he?"

As the hairless skin in my armpits twitched, Mom's face crimped like a persimmon.

"Your son is not slow. He's solidly in the fifth percentile."

"Fifth percentile?"

"Look at the big picture. Over 10,000 children have passed through this office on their way to adulthood on my watch. At least 5%—500 slow growers—have grown all the way up, enough to fill the gymnasium of any high school in Ashleigh."

Dr. Wise dispensed a big wink in plain view of the patient.

"We'll not be in the bottom fifth percentile of anything," huffed Mom. "I want a second opinion."

"Mother," exhaled Dr. Wise through bristle-lipped nostrils. "Ma'am. I rarely solicit outside assistance."

"When the situation calls, whom do you call?"

"Your husband is in training at the medical college," said Dr. Wise through a cleared throat, "isn't he?"

"He's never around," said Mom.

"Specializing in obstetrics, if I'm not mistaken?"

Dad declared he wanted to be around happy events. I guess I couldn't blame him. Six years earlier, after our family moved from New Jersey to North Carolina, Mom had trouble moving in. While Dad chucked a repeatedly relocated career in polymers to start medical school so he could be his own boss, Mom washed her hands, or fell asleep, or woke up and made my little sister, Leah, our dog, Snorty, and me scour our peeling rental house for a college yearbook, an eyebrow pencil, or another bar of soap. Although Dad professed 31-year-old medical students could shoulder lots of loans, Mom wrung her hands that much more over a missing war bond, a gift from her father for winning a grade school spelling bee. If we found no buried treasure, Mom stayed stationary and cried. At age eight, I was too old, but Leah cried, too.

One morning, I walked in on Mom as she gazed into her hand mirror at the kitchen table. She turned her head to me and back to the mirror before she said, "You." Then she smashed the mirror against the tabletop, clutched the largest piece in her right hand, and slashed her left wrist. A pulse of blood splashed on my face.

Help! My mouth formed the word, but it wouldn't come out. Help! "Help!" At last. I spat it out.

The blood dribbled along the table.

Who could hear? Dad was at school, Snorty outside, and Leah in never-never land.

I ran next door, brushed tears and blood from my face, listened to Old Lady Antonelli call me "Francis," convinced her I wasn't bleeding, and listened to her call Mom an ambulance.

Dad called me a brave little man. After Mom's stitches and shock treatments, he went on to thank me for freeing him to pursue his studies, since these things take time, especially when it came time for Mom to come home.

I swore to myself I'd put up with anything so as not to inspire Mom to put on a repeat performance.

With my dark hair and broad nose (minus a deep voice), Dad even said I took after him. Given that Mom (in the course of her recovery) acquired a button nose, bonded teeth, and bleached hair, Dad must have been right.

"Yes," said Mom. "My husband is learning how to secure babies."

"I thought so," said Dr. Wise without winking. "After all, I've been treating you with professional courtesy."

Mom fell mum. With the exception of Lady Clairol, every practitioner in Ashleigh treated her with professional courtesy, as well as Southern hospitality.

"So you see, ma'am, your husband is in a better position than I to seek a second opinion."

———— ✦ ————

"There is something wrong with him," said Mom. "I just know it."

As Mom repeated the story of my life, I sat naked, but for a white paper gown, on the examining table of Dr. Hatley Finkel.

"Rest assured, Mrs. Rose, we will employ the latest medical advances." The Chief of Pediatric Endocrinology at Carolina Medical College, with whom Dad lined me up, undoubtedly plied nothing less than state-of-the-art. Still, the pointed tufts of hair on the sides of his otherwise bald skull had to be pilfered from a prehistoric Plymouth's tail fins.

"That's what we want," affirmed the one who cherished me more than our barren rock garden. "No stone unturned."

One week remained before my first undressing before the jocks at Charlie "Choo Choo" Justice High School.

"I think we can eliminate the element of surprise," said an

oval, smile-shellacked head self-simonized by fingers grafted from the tendrils of an eggplant. "Franklin, remove your gown."

By using my first name, albeit the rotten formal one, Dr. Finkel and his starched white coat assumed we were pals. When would he tell Mom—the way Dr. Wise always did—to step out of the room? "No cause for modesty, son."

Now we were related. Meanwhile, Mom railed against Leah's persistent baby fat, Dad's persistent baby fat, the latest maid she axed for stealing her war bond, her battle with depression, and the dangers of turning anger inward.

"Nothing we haven't seen before," said Dr. Finkel.

Yes, but it had been ages since Mom and Dad gave me a bath.

"Besides, we need to start on the same page, so we can monitor your progress."

We? I pulled the gown over my head and crossed one leg over the other, turning my crotch into the triangular crease of a girl.

"Lie down flat, my boy."

"Can't you refer to Dr. Wise's growth chart?" I said.

"That's a little simpleminded, son. Uncross your legs."

"What about her?"

After Mom stood up, Dr. Finkel's cold hands spread my knees apart.

"See. Nothing to it."

My eyes froze shut as frigid feelers crawled over my belly.

"The liver span is acceptable. The spleen likewise isn't enlarged. Oh, and he has an outie."

"Is that an acceptable enlargement?" asked Mom, peering.

"Yes," said Dr. Finkel.

I squeezed my hands into fists. Something new but still below zero hopped on my skin.

"The lungs are clear. The heart is without murmurs.

Nonetheless, he has audible bowel sounds."

"Is that good?" asked Mom.

"Yes," said Dr. Finkel.

I wished I could cut a good fart.

"Let's check him for hernias."

A cold pointy thing delved into the right side of my sac.

"Cough, Franklin, cough."

I did as told.

The cold pointy thing dove to the left.

"Again."

Again.

"That's a good boy."

It's hard work being a good boy.

"As you can see, Mrs. Rose, there are no hernias."

"Yes, I see."

With the worst surely over, I opened my eyes. Dr. Finkel, Mom, and a metal device stolen from a shoe store hovered over the wrong appendage. Dr. Finkel took hold of my right nut between his thumb and forefinger and placed it on the platter. He compressed the instrument's length and width until my teeth curled before performing an encore, stage left.

"What's his size?" asked Mom through cracks caked with lipstick.

"Inconclusive," said Dr. Finkel as a band of sweat collected on his brow. Either that or I had managed to whiz on him.

"Is there a way to tell?" said Mom.

"Not without more data."

Oblivious to Dr. Wise's grading scale, Dr. Finkel pried open another cabinet and produced an apparatus for weighing meat at a butcher shop, except it sported a lady wearing a blindfold.

"Kneel."

"Huh?"

"As in prayer."

I turned my head toward Mom and pleaded for mercy with

my eyes.

"We appreciate thoroughness, Dr. Finkel."

I sat up, considered jumping off the table and running out of the room, realized I was naked, and considered jumping off the table and running out of the room.

"Put your back into it," said Dr. Finkel.

The paper on the examining table crackled under my knees.

"More."

Although they refused to retract, my cold shrunken balls, to their credit, resisted hanging like wattles.

"More."

Was he positioning me for a guillotine?

"That'll do."

My gonads rested, one apiece, on each side of the Scales of Justice. Dr. Finkel flicked a doohickey before writing down his findings.

"Stop leaning."

"Does that mean I can put on my clothes?"

"Hang in there, son. One can never have too much data."

Along those lines, Dr. Finkel whipped a dog-eared strip of tape out of his pocket and measured my pee shooter from end to end.

"Where can we get one of those?" asked Mom.

"They go for next to nothing almost anywhere," said Dr. Finkel. "One more thing, and the inventory will be complete."

I didn't know I had any more things.

"Turn on your side."

"Come again?"

"Toward the wall."

As Dr. Finkel snapped a rubber glove in place, I found myself lying face-to-face with his diplomas.

"This will take only a second."

I howled for more than the second it took.

"You'll be heartened to hear, Mrs. Rose, Franklin has a

readily palpable prostate. Go ahead and get dressed, son, while your mother and I are in conference."

After the conferees receded, I clawed into my clothes before anyone else could see. Silly me. Except for the framed photograph of Nixon, Dr. Finkel's waiting room was deserted. I hunted for hidden things in a picture in the only magazine.

Over an hour passed before the huddle broke.

"I believe your boy is suitable for high school," stated Dr. Finkel, "but these things take time. We will need to see him back here to corroborate our findings on a regular basis."

"Nothing will stand in our way," said Mom.

I made a secret vow to stand in front of a runaway truck, culminating in an impenetrable body cast.

"Good things come in small packages," said Dr. Finkel.

"We can't thank you enough," gushed Mom, replicating Dr. Finkel's grin for the road. "Now we're ready. But just to be sure, we'll keep a close eye on things."

During the search for our subcompact in the sweltering parking lot outside Carolina Medical College, Mom finally sought my opinion.

A CONVERSATION WITH ROBERT GARNER MCBREARTY

Lowestoft Chronicle, November 2015

Robert Garner McBrearty
(Photography: Norman L. Rheme)

In the early Eighties, while working as a dishwasher in a restaurant, Robert Garner Mcbrearty, an MFA graduate of the Iowa Writers' Workshop, achieved a major literary triumph when his first published story was selected for the prestigious Pushcart Prize anthology. Since then, he's picked up numerous writing awards, published three critically-acclaimed story collections, and seen his fiction appear in major literary publications like *North American Review, Missouri Review, New England Review, Narrative Magazine, StoryQuarterly*, and *Mississippi Review*. This October saw the long-overdue publication of his debut novel, *The Western Lonesome Society*, which has been some fifteen years in the making.

In an exclusive, in-depth interview with *Lowestoft Chronicle*, Robert Garner McBrearty discusses his poignant and humorous novel, the early days of his writing career, the Iowa Writers' Workshop, and the origins of many of his characters and short stories.

"Worthy of Ares..."
David Weddersl, author of The Story of Edgar Sawtelle

THE WESTERN
LONESOME SOCIETY
A NOVEL
ROBERT GARNER MCBREARTY

The Western Lonesome Society
Conundrum Press, 2015

Lowestoft Chronicle (LC): Robert, I read *The Western Lonesome Society* earlier this month and thought it was spectacular. It's hilarious, touching, exhilarating, disturbing, profound, and entirely unique. You've drawn from your previous short stories in terms of themes (mental illness, kidnapping, etc.) and characters, but you've tied diverse material together through various clever means and, to paraphrase the character Dave, the skillful creative writing student, "jazzed it up a little." Did this novel emerge from your short story "Let the Birds Drink in Peace" or did you later decide to incorporate the story? Considering the stories within stories element, the numerous unrelated characters, and differing time periods, how challenging was it fashioning a coherent plot?

Robert Garner McBrearty (RGM): "Let the Birds Drink in Peace" actually was always in the novel and I thought that with some modifications, it would work as a short story, so I lifted that section for use as a story in the collection of that same title. But it was always very central to the novel as it introduces Jim O'Brien and his parents and siblings and their lives growing up in Texas. I would say that the novel really built from this section and from the initial kidnapping of the boys by the Comanches. Those two happenings were what I first had, sort of working side by side, the ancestors kidnapped by the Comanches and Jim's kidnapping in 1960. I had those elements, but I didn't know how they fit together… "Fashioning a coherent plot" is probably why it took me so long to write this book, not in its first draft, which took about six months, but almost fifteen years in the rewriting! Not working on it consistently, though.

During that time, I worked on a lot of other stories and novels and I was teaching a lot, and I would set *Lonesome* (originally titled *Notes to My Literary Agent*) aside for long periods of time before coming back to it. But the central problem was fitting things together coherently—I think, now, there actually is a coherent structure, though I'm not sure everyone would agree with that!

Maybe I should explain how I got started on the book. I had just published my first collection of stories, *A Night at the Y*. I think after one publishes his first book, the question arises: *What now?* I wanted to try something different, but I didn't know what. I decided that my approach, as an experiment, would be to just go to a coffee shop every day, or almost every day, and just write for a couple of hours and see what emerged, not worrying about how anything connected. After a while, I think the mind has an instinctive urge to start making connections and coherence, and I realized I couldn't just babble on day after day, but needed some way of focusing. I mentioned the original title earlier, *Notes to My Literary Agent,* and that title indicates my original concept: It would be about a writer writing to his agent (an imaginary agent, actually) proposing various novel ideas, some of which were ridiculous. Actually, in my short story "After Zombies" we see some of this agent/writer interplay, so I find it interesting that, over the years, there are certain ideas that emerge again and again. But two of the novel ideas that Jim, the protagonist and narrator, comes up with are his own kidnapping and the kidnapping of his ancestors. So those two story ideas started to travel parallel paths, at first extremely sketchy, but they began to flush out—I should back up here a bit, and come back to this later. At the time, I was also reading quite a bit of frontier history and no doubt that played into why I was drawn to writing about the brothers kidnapped by the Comanches. Originally, there was a lot more of Jim as a writer and his interactions with his agent, but it seemed too much like a writer writing about writing, and while there is still some of that in the novel, I think it's a lot less about that now. We see Jim start to write about something perhaps, but then I want the reader to forget about that and just get into the actual story.

I would say that there's one main theme in the book and several lesser themes and various ways of connecting the various stories-within-stories. I kept asking myself the question: *What's this book really all about?* And I started to think about how many kidnappings there are in the story—the kids in Texas in 1960, Jim's mother's brief abduction by Roughhound, the ancestors kidnapped by the Comanches. Dave, the student, is kidnapped in Mexico. People are taken from their homes, displaced, and the question arises of how to get back home, and where is home anyway, so I realized it was a novel about looking for belonging. Our central character Jim feels adrift in his own neighborhood and in his life at the university, so as he's telling the story, he's also looking for his own way to belong. We even see, at one point, Jim has mysteriously ended up in Paris with Ernest Hemingway, way away from his own home. Anyway, discovering that central theme of belonging and searching for home helped a great deal in connecting the various threads. It made it possible to go off in different directions because there was some core that held it all together.

You mentioned the various means of bringing things together—yes, a great question. It didn't all come together at once, but various connecting means started coming to me. One was the reason why Jim is writing about his ancestors, and I realized it was because his mother had encouraged him to. Realizing that helped me a whole lot because it gives Jim some motivation to be writing about that. It took me, oddly enough, a long time to realize that when it should have been so obvious because my own mother had always encouraged me to write about our family history, which did include life on the Texas frontier, though my own ancestors were not kidnapped. After that, I saw the clear trajectory of the boys' story, from their kidnapping, to their return, to their difficult readjustments. In some ways, that part was probably the easiest to write because I saw that plot thread very clearly.

Partly, it was a matter of figuring out motivation. For instance, I started writing Dave the student's wild tale, but at first I didn't realize the importance to Jim, who is reading it. But it was when the student suggests Jim "jazz up" his own stories that I saw why it was important to Jim. He starts viewing his own writing as maybe a little dull and he needs to jazz it up. That idea of "jazzing it up" is actually being used throughout. Even the RV trip, which starts as a dull depiction of a trip, ends up being jazzed up.

Another element that helped me a lot was what I think of as "returning points." We return several times to Jim in his office above the garage, talking to his imaginary therapist about his problems, and returning as well to his university office and being confronted by his foe, the mad linguist Dr. Dalton. Those "returns" are helpful in keeping things together. As a writer, I could even sort of say to myself, ah, here we are again.

One of the biggest problems was the opening. It took me a long time to write the first chapter, as it now exists. There was always something wrong with the opening, which was that I was playing it too straight at first, so that readers weren't prepared for the type of novel it would be. I think what I needed to do was to let the reader in on what type of novel they could expect, so with the imaginary therapist and the imagined scene about winning the Nobel, I let the reader in on it, that it's going to be a wild sort of ride, with various story threads, and by doing that, I give myself a certain freedom to tell the tale. It's sort of like telling the reader: "This is going to be a little crazy. Hang on!" By doing that, already a kind of coherence is created since one is expecting the wild ride.

LC: I really liked the idea of the linguist, Dr. Dalton, and the way Jim is antagonized by him even when he isn't physically there—a flashcard with letters on it being enough to set Jim off. Unlike the imaginary therapist, there are no descriptions of Dalton (and President Jammer has less of a presence). Did you have someone in mind when you came up with Dalton's character? In your original draft, were there more scenes with either of these characters that didn't make it to the finished version?

RGM: I had a lot of fun creating those characters. I wouldn't say they're drawn from specific individuals, but they're composites of academic types, drawn to exaggerated proportions. It's interesting that you ask whether there were originally more scenes with Dr. Dalton and President Jammer because that is the case. I mentioned earlier that the writing of the book took fifteen years, and Dr. Dalton and President Jammer kind of floated in and out of the drafts—in some drafts being given more weight, in some drafts less. I was trying to figure out how much weight they should have in the book. My thinking about them became really intensified in the last few years because, by that time, my relationship with the university had become estranged. I think all in all I was a good teacher—I'd like to think so anyway. But I was never really an academic type—I was a writer who happened to be making a living teaching but who didn't really care too much about academia and didn't have the good grace to pretend to be. But anyway, I think that sense of estrangement got distilled down into those two characters. I remember walks across campus, carrying this heavy cloth briefcase, and in the morning, especially when it was quiet, I'd imagine this pale gas creeping out from the bushes. Maybe it's working anywhere too long, but you can have this sense of slipping into mediocrity, and in a way the gas represented that—something that would just stultify you if you weren't stultified enough already. I think the consciousness is a little like that—we wake up a bit, perk up, look about, get excited, and then something makes us lose that wide awake feeling and we dull out. Creativity is like that, and I think that's what was haunting me the last few years there at the university, this feeling that my creativity as a writer was being stultified by the teaching and the assortment of other tasks.

In some of the earlier drafts, Jammer was doing more, sending out harassing notes to the faculty and things like that, and there was more interplay between Jim and his students and co-workers, but it began to feel too much like I was writing about academia and that really wasn't the direction I wanted to go in, so I distilled Jammer down essentially to the sender of the gas. That seemed to say it all, really, what I wanted to say about Jim and his relationship with the university.

I think with Dr. Dalton, also, I wasn't thinking about one person in particular. I was thinking about people who get under your skin, who are not there to help you in life but to thwart you. Being given to comedic exaggeration, it popped into my head that there was a guy who could get to you, not just verbally, but could go after you from any direction, sneak words into your reading material that would drive you into a frenzy. As a writer, of course, Jim deals with language, so attacking him through his reading material is one of the most destructive things someone can do. I think what both Jammer and Dalton do is to create this feeling like Jim is under assault, and we see at the end, finally, that he's not going to take it anymore, he's going to give Jammer the "fisherman's toss" out the window.

As I said, it took a lot of drafts to figure out, but ultimately I opted to just keep them in a little so that the university becomes more backdrop than heavily focused on. At the same time, I had great fun having my say about the university. It's almost sort of a mythical place to me, the university, and Jammer and Dalton are a bit mythical, too, kind of off-screen presences, especially Jammer. I liked their brief appearances, along the lines of the "returning points" I spoke of earlier. But I think it was the right choice to downplay them. Sometimes less makes more.

LC: Comanches appear in many of your previous short stories—sometimes the references are minor, sometimes they're central to the story, as with the bipolar character Len in "Episodes" who's fixated on his family's frontier days (graphically recounting his great-great Uncle Ira's extraordinary and brutal dealings with them). They feature heavily in this novel too—one of the main story threads concerns tribe leader White Crane and the shattering impact he has on a family when he abducts their two young boys and integrates them into his tribe, becoming a surrogate father to them. You've obviously done a great deal of historical research into the tribe. How atypical is Will and Tom's story? And, as a father of two boys yourself, was it at all unsettling writing these scenes or, for that matter, a chapter like "The Stalker"?

RGM: Wonderful question. Well, my family history dates back to Texas in the 1850s, so I think I've always been interested in the frontier days. My mother's grandmother had a small ranch in Texas and my mother would tell tales that she recalled. As well, I've always enjoyed reading frontier history and I've read various captivity narratives of people who were taken by the Comanches. While I'm not trying to write a historical novel, the experience of Tom and Will was not unique. If children, especially boys, were accepted by the tribe, they often adjusted to their lives with the Indians, and if they were returned, they often wanted to go back to the Indians. The younger one was, the more likely that one would view the Indians as his real family. In Will's case, as the younger brother, he very much feels like he belongs with the Comanches. Tom, the older one, has enough memory of his real home to be torn. Though White Crane has taken the boys, I wanted to present him as a kind character and a good father, in his own way, to the boys. Will fully accepts him; Tom is always ambivalent.

I'm glad you brought up my own children because no doubt that was a big influence. Children and siblings are important in this novel. I remember around the time I started the novel, there were reports in the news about kids who'd been kidnapped and then who had been found, years later, living with some other family. So I think that was on my mind, and I was pretty protective about my kids—I don't think fanatically so—but as I was writing about the kidnappings, I did find myself entering into the story, becoming pretty anxious and melancholy at times. Now that I think about it, parts of the novel—not all— are on the sad side, and writing about sad things probably does make me sad. It was disturbing to write those scenes! Maybe it was a relief when I would come back to the funny parts, which kind of alternate throughout the novel—sad, funny, sad, funny, both sad and funny.

LC: One of the advantages of this longer format is that it helped you to develop some of the comic elements—Jim's hilariously wild sessions with his blunt, vulgar, perverted therapist, for example, or Jim's student, Dave, and his captivating tale of his love affair with a deranged stripper. That "reversal" technique you've mentioned in reference to your story "The Dishwasher" is also present when Jim recounts his outrageous family summer vacation as allegedly "pure memoir." The mix of zany humor and dark, touching moments seem to work very well. Did you make a conscious effort to create this funny yet poignant quality to your writing, or did it naturally come out that way?

RGM: I'm glad you found the sections with the therapist hilarious! I really had fun writing those sections. One of my own brothers is a therapist, a good one, not at all like this guy, but my brother is probably one of my reasons for being interested in mental health subjects. I'm glad you brought up my short stories because this novel is both an extension of those and something different as well. I think, as a short story writer, I've worked the range—everything from stories that are mostly comedic, to dark ones, to ones that are both funny and serious, from the experimental to the traditional, from the realistic to the absurd. I think in this book, I pulled on all of that. The longer form provided a great opportunity to work the full gamut. I'd say rather than a conscious effort, it was more like what came to me, what felt right at the time, and you know, as I think about it, it really was like I was going into whatever mood I was writing about—if the scene was sad, I was sad. Or maybe it was the reverse—I was sad, so the scene was sad? I will say this: I think I poured more of myself into that book than into anything else I've written, and in doing that, maybe the duality of the book—the mix of funny and sad—more fully comes out in the longer form. I had a blast writing this book, especially the funnier parts, and I hope it's a blast for the readers, too. And, at times, I was very melancholic writing it, and maybe that comes through, too.

LC: What made you want to be a fiction writer, Robert? Does your passion for literature stem from childhood or was it formed later? (I believe I read somewhere that you started writing as a teenager.) And when did you first start submitting your work for publication? What was the first piece you had published?

RGM: Oh man, I like this question, but it makes me feel really old, too. My mother was a huge reader and she always encouraged me to read, and I loved to read as a kid, so I think my writing life really started with that—with my mother reading to me and then encouraging me to read. Freshman year in high school, 1968, in English class, Brother Al—I went to a Catholic school—told us to write a short story. I wrote, of all things, a Western with a twist. I enjoyed the hell out of the assignment, and I was hooked. I decided right then and there—fourteen years old—I was going to be a writer. My mother thought it was great. My father, to his credit, thought it was good, but advised me to keep an eye out for a backup line of work.

I won a couple of writing contests in college, one at San Antonio Community College and one at the University of Texas. I started submitting stories and poems to literary magazines when I was nineteen, and I probably wrote a couple of hundred stories, but I didn't get my first story accepted until I was twenty-eight (other than one that appeared in the community college newspaper). God only knows, I know something about persistence. Then that first story "The Dishwasher" was accepted by *Mississippi Review* in 1982, and then was taken for the Pushcart Prize. That felt huge, being included in Pushcart, especially for my first published story. At the time, I actually had a job washing dishes, so being a dishwasher with a story in Pushcart about being a dishwasher gave me a certain prestige at the restaurant. Or as the restaurant owner's wife said to me: "You've got a Master's degree in English and a published story and here you are washing dishes. You must really be stupid." But the acceptance definitely was a big boost.

Interestingly enough, "The Dishwasher" still gets some attention. It's been reprinted here and there, an excerpt was used in Janet Burroway's popular book, *Writing Fiction*, and just last year, a high school drama club adapted it for stage and it won the Maine Drama Festival.

LC: The literary quality present in your writing makes your stories perfect candidates for those well-regarded university journals like *North American Review*, *Missouri Review*, *Mississippi Review*, and *New England Review*, all of which you've been published in. To what extent did the Iowa Writers' Workshop influence your writing?

RGM: All in all, the Writers' Workshop was a good experience for me, though how much it influenced me, I'm not entirely sure. What it did give me, I think, was a thicker skin, which I definitely needed. Prior to the Workshop, I was under the illusion that everyone loved my writing and always would. I sort of suspect that many of the students go there with similar expectations, or at least maybe they did back then. So it was sort of a shock—ultimately a healthy one—to realize that there were a lot of other good writers around and that I was going to need to work damn hard to have half a chance as a writer.

I think I got a little self-conscious about my writing when I was there. The critique sessions could be pretty tough, and I think I felt a little restrained by that—afraid of taking chances, which worked against my inclination to cut loose. In fact, I wrote "The Dishwasher" one night after working at the Hamburg Inn, a kind of iconic Iowa City diner. I figured the class would trash it for being kind of silly or something, so I never showed it in the workshop, and I've always been glad about that, as I probably would have screwed it up trying to rewrite it or, worse, maybe just discarded it. As it was, it lingered around on my desk in various places until one day I reread it and thought it was pretty funny and I thought, "Southerners have a sense of humor. I'll try the *Mississippi Review*."

I might sound a little negative about the Workshop, but I don't really mean to be because I think I am a better writer as a result. I got tougher on myself, and I learned something about rewriting. And there were people there who liked my writing quite a bit and were very encouraging. Plus, the degree itself has been helpful. I didn't use it for five years after I got out. I just worked odd jobs—I'm glad I did that, but it was hard. The degree, along with my publications, helped me start getting some teaching gigs, which were a lot better than washing dishes, fond as I am of that profession. So the workshop was good in its own way, but it was also good that I kind of put it behind me and did things my own way, without worrying too much. I find the more I cut loose, follow my own lead, the better I do.

LC: Considering how highly regarded the Iowa Writer' Workshop is and how, of the hundreds of fiction candidates who apply, only about twenty-five are accepted, how thrilling was it to get into the program? Part of the application process entails submitting a manuscript. What did you submit?

RGM: You know, it was strange, actually. At the time, I didn't really know how significant it was to be accepted. I mean, I did know of the reputation, but I was twenty-five, living in Mexico at the time, teaching English, and I was pretty happy with what I was doing, though in the back of my mind I'd always thought it would be a good idea to go to graduate school. A couple of older writer friends, Leonard Robinson, who was both a good friend and a sort of mentor to me, and his wife, the poet Patricia Goedicke, encouraged me to apply to Iowa. By this time, I'd already had a fellowship to the MacDowell Colony. I was twenty-three when I went to MacDowell, I think one of the youngest ones ever, so I wasn't all that surprised when I got accepted into Iowa. I know that sounds arrogant, but it was really more that I was somewhat oblivious. The real shock was when I got there and I gathered shortly that there were plenty of good writers there, and some pretty tough critics, not really mean ones, but it might have felt a bit like that at the time.

For my application, I submitted the first few chapters of a novel-in-progress titled *The Coffee Drinker*. It got me in, but the novel pretty much got trashed in the workshops. Probably if I went back and read it again, I'd agree with the reaction. I remember a depressing talk with one of my teachers who said, more or less, that it was going to be a long haul for me. My second year, I switched back to short stories and I did better with those. I actually had sort of my own following who were really into my stories. They were the ones who were printing out the stories for the workshops and they said my stories always made them laugh so they were always looking forward to them. I'd gone from overconfidence to insecurity, and that little informal group, as well as a couple of close friends, and a couple of teachers, helped counter the insecurity.

As I said earlier, though, all in all it was a good experience and I'm glad I went there.

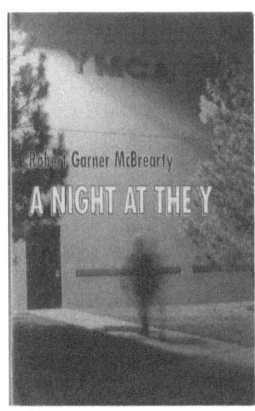

A Night at the Y
John Daniel & Company, 1999

LC: How closely do you draw on personal experience when developing characters, situations, and dialogue? I'm thinking here not just of stories like "The Acting Class," "The Pearl Diver," or "The Dishwasher," but of many others where the focus is on issues related to childhood or fatherhood or some sense of missed opportunity, regrets, failures, remembrances of heroic actions, etc.?

RGM: That's a question I often ask myself. Where do characters come from? How closely do the "I" characters in my stories resemble the real true living "I"? And, even if I am writing in a third person voice, how close are those characters to me? The question also arises of how closely other characters in the stories are based on real people or experiences. I think the answer is a complicated one. I am reminded of something Tennessee Williams said about his characters, I think especially in regard to *A Streetcar Named Desire*. He said that all his characters were essentially manifestations of different aspects of himself. I wouldn't go that far, but I would say the "self," anyone's self, contains many "selves." The bad guy walks alongside the good guy, the coward walks alongside the hero. Maybe a bit of Jungian psychology applies here. Often, at least some part of myself inhabits the main characters and maybe even the other characters.

When I look at most of my stories, I can usually see something from my own experiences that sparked the stories. Sometimes, there's a very close resemblance to real life. For instance, in "The Pearl Diver," I really was washing dishes at the time I wrote it and I was in a relationship with a young woman quite a bit like the woman in the story, who actually became my wife—and still is, these thirty or so years later! It was kind of a tough time for me. I was a couple of years out of grad school, dead broke, washing dishes (soon to find out I'd won a Pushcart for my other story about washing dishes at a different restaurant a couple of years before), and the relationship was the best thing I had going. The story was very much about trying to find hope: "I'm just trying to talk ourselves some place nice," the character says to his girlfriend. As in the story, in real life, I would do some spoofs at work to amuse my fellow employees about how I was ranked the number two dishwasher in the country and needed to be number one to win the affections of my girl, but in the story I exaggerated all that quite a bit. I'd also say the character in the story was more naïve and hopeful than I really was as a young man. The story did mirror real life quite a bit—a relationship, a near break up, a reuniting, heading forth into the future together. And, yet, there is an exaggerated quality to the story. Even in the stories closest to the bone, there's something at least somewhat fictitious either about the main character or the circumstances. The closest I've come to pure memoir is probably "The Things I Don't Know About," which recounts, in part, my mother's illness and passing and my attempt during that time to write some of our family history in order to please her. Wow, you know in writing this, I just made a connection that that story probably had something to do with the later writing of *The Western Lonesome Society*.

I think that "The Pearl Diver" is my most hopeful story, the least unambiguous. I don't think I'm a "dark" writer in general; that is, I'm not someone who is overly cynical. At least, I see beauty and goodness in the world, the possibility of that anyway, and yet most of the stories are weighted, even the funny ones like "After Zombies," with some sense that the characters have, referring to your question, suffered from missed opportunities, regrets, failures, remembrances of heroic actions, and also heroic actions not taken. Part of this probably stems out of the nature of being a writer—you know, hardly any of us hit the great glory that we maybe dreamed of when we set out to be writers, and even those that do often discover it wasn't what they in mind—they're even gloomier and more messed up than ever. Fame and riches don't seem to solve much—though I wouldn't mind having a minor go at it to see if I do any better at it. On the flip side, I have a wildly optimistic streak, which might be given voice by Jim's imagining of winning the Nobel and wondering if it will be okay if he plays himself in the miniseries. In real life, I will actually find myself kind of chuckling and grinning to myself as I imagine things like that happening. A little fantasizing doesn't hurt; maybe it helps stir one onward.

But as I've gotten older, I think that my own disappointments (don't get me wrong, I've had some very rewarding things, too) weigh on me some and that disappointment inhabits some of the characters. I'm sure that same sense of disappointment is true of many professions—why wasn't I the best salesman? Why did my team lose so many games?

Failures to act in some situations haunt me. In real life, I've been lucky enough to pull off a couple of rescues. I don't think I'll go into that here, but rather than feeling good about it, I was always aware of how close I came to *not* doing the action. And for the rare times of taking the action, I think of all the times I haven't—where I should have spoken up or done something differently. My story "The Helmeted Man" describes an incident where a man is thought to have done a heroic deed, rescued a woman who is being robbed at an ATM machine, but eventually, the man begins to doubt what happened—maybe it was more of an accident that he'd helped her rather than a heroic action.

That kind of thinking comes front and center when you're thinking about your own family, "should have done this, should have done that." I'd say Jim O'Brien, for instance, in *Lonesome,* is haunted by those feelings of inadequacy as a father. I think that's where the crazy part in Spain stems from, where he punches out the cop and rescues his son—sort of his way, maybe, of saying, here, damn it, at least in this part of the story I'm going to save the day! I think the sense of failure, in part anyway, isn't even about whether one is a good or bad parent—certainly there are degrees—but the failure, the impossibility, really, of being able to protect your kids when they're out in the world. I drew on that feeling when I created the father, Edmund, who is searching for his sons who have been taken by the Comanches. Edmund isn't in the story all that much, but I felt very close to that character, could relate to his sadness and despair.

Tom and Will, the kidnapped kids, are sort of based on my own two sons—poor kids, I had them get kidnapped by the

Comanches! I kind of felt guilty about that. The dynamic sort of matches up—the older, responsible one, and the younger, sort of wilder one. And then they show up in other forms in the trip to Spain and in the RV trip.

Sometimes, the connection to my actual experience is much more tenuous. Let's take the story "Houston, 1984," for example. The main character there is working as a private detective. Never happened. I did have a friend who said he'd briefly worked as a private detective and followed people around, mostly to catch adulterous affairs. He said it sickened him to do that. I put a character somewhat like myself into the main role. I'd had a boss at a completely different job who was a real sleaze and he became the model for the arrogant, sleazy head of the agency. You mentioned dialogue, and the boss in that story spoke very much in the sort of grandiose self-serving style of that real-life boss I had. Other times, I don't know—I just kind of start hearing the dialogue in my mind. It has to come out of the character somehow to be real, not to be invented from the outside.

I think my writing of dialogue has been influenced by my acting background, which wasn't extensive, but I was in drama in high school and in college, and I think inhabiting other characters on stage helped me to get inside the heads of my characters and hearing them talk. That is, I feel like they're doing the talking and I'm just writing it down. I hear their voices and the voices are often mixed in with visual imagery, as if we might be on stage together and I'm simultaneously actor, writer, director, audience, but though it's theatrical, at the same time it feels very real to me. Yet, yet—there's always a "yet"—there's also another part of me that has enough distance to get it all down on the page, or maybe it's the director who takes over and says, "No, no, that's not quite right, try it again."

Coming back to *The Western Lonesome Society* for a moment. The main character Jim O'Brien feels a lot like me, and yet he isn't exactly "me." He teaches at a university, which I did. He views the university somewhat as an absurd place, which I did. That isn't to say that I did a bad job or that I look down upon academia in general, just that I found some aspects of it to be absurd, or maybe I was the absurd one in a sane university. But I didn't want to get into a big depiction of academia, so I just made up two elements—President Jammer who releases a gas every so often to keep the students and faculty in line, and Dr. Dalton, a mad linguist. They only show up a couple of times, but I think it's enough to create Jim's sense of the absurd.

The three young O'Briens who are kidnapped in the beginning bear a resemblance to my older brother and to my sister, and the parents bear a resemblance to my actual parents. The incident of being kidnapped never happened, and yet when I wrote it, it felt very real. It made me kind of nervous. You know what's very real? The backyard in that story. I see that so clearly, from when we first moved into that house in the early Sixties, when it was just a mud and colichi yard, to the way it looks now, full of trees, a jungly garden. The backyard shows up in "Episode" and in other stories, as well.

One thing I try to do with characters is to spread the wealth around, so to speak. That is, let's say I have a main character. I like that main character to feed off the story to the other characters—let them speak, let a lot of the story come through them. That was one thing I liked in the writing of *Western*, how many characters I created.

LC: There are a lot of characters in *Western*, now you mention it. I like how varied they are, and how they all seem to have a purpose to the plot. In terms of some of your characters, I want to ask about a couple outside of this novel. As with "The Helmeted Man," Ralph, the central character in "A Night at The Y," is also reminiscing about a heroic deed. But what I love about this story is that, by the end of his frenzied night, he continues to play the hero. And then there's the hellraiser, like the one in "Back in Town" and Scooter in "The Hellraiser," who are either unable or unwilling to curb their disruptive behavior. How do you get into the mindset of these diverse characters? Do you identify more with someone like Ralph than Scooter? And how do you make a rough, hard drinking, womanizing, looting, bank robber so damn endearing?

RGM: I think I'll start with "The Hellraiser" because the genesis of that one comes back very clearly to me. I was about twenty-eight. I was living in Santa Fe at the time, but I'd come back to San Antonio for Christmas, and I went to a bar with my younger brother and with two friends. I think we went to a series of bars actually, and one of them was a strip joint. I was engaged to be married and I didn't have any big desire to stay out, but one of my friends insisted we stay out longer. That friend is the model for Scooter in the story. The story really came to me when "Scooter" in real life put his arm around a waitress and said, "This is my life. This is what I live for." There it was, the whole hellraiser philosophy distilled into that quote. We know that Scooter is doomed in a sense, doomed to repeat the same patterns. Sometimes you know you have a story. It's forming in your mind and you know you have it. I turned the story over to Scooter, put it in his point of view, used the more folksy, Texan-y voice of my friend. He's making both a defense of his own behavior and an underlying admission that he knows he's doomed, but maybe there's a slight misplaced nobility in that he's sticking true to himself. Of course, as I'm allowing Scooter to tell the story, there's a part of me in there, too.

You've noticed that theme in "Back in Town" as well, the character unable or unwilling to curb his destructive behavior, and that's certainly a theme that interests me. Maybe because I've been a bit close to that edge myself, not to be overly dramatic. I think we all have some split between our earlier years and the sort of person we end up being. But let's say it seemed like my life was headed in one direction—off to Mexico at the age of twenty-one, then some years of odd jobs mixed with school, town to town, and then somewhere along the way, passing through Santa Fe, I end up living out "The Pearl Diver" story, meeting the woman who's been my lifelong companion and we raise kids and live kind of a quiet life in suburbia, so these days I identify more with the quiet family man Ralph in "A Night at the Y." But we see in Ralph that he draws upon the old side of himself, too, summons it up to help out the family, so the earlier hellraising self isn't always a bad thing.

I go back to those "turning point" stories again and again. Characters are either going to turn for the better or not make the turn. I think in "Back in Town" what we see is someone who has almost made the turn and a part of him would really like to be good, but he's just slipping lower, one step at a time, and we know it's probably inevitable. At the same time, he's self-reporting in a way that is both comical and desperate, so maybe that helps readers like him, even if we know his actual behavior is all wrong. I think in fiction we can like characters even if we wouldn't think much of that sort of person in real life. We can be a lot more forgiving and tolerant of fictional characters. To be honest, I'd bar the door now if someone like Scooter showed up.

LC: One of my favorite stories by you is "Colonel Travis's Lament," from your second collection *Let the Birds Drink In Peace*. Your wonderful depictions of fabled characters like Davy Crockett ("The most self-serving egomaniac you've ever met") and James Bowie ("he had a way of eying your chest as if he were thinking of sticking his huge knife there") suggest you had fun writing about them. In an earlier story, "My Life as a

Let the Birds Drink in Peace
Conundrum Press, 2011

Judo Master," the character Sean is "enamored with tales of the Alamo" and acts out battle scenes with his older brother. Like Sean, were you fascinated by stories of the Alamo as a child? Did you have any reservations about taking on big personalities like Crockett? Are there other famous historical figures you've considered writing about?

RGM: As you've noticed, I was indeed "enamored with tales of the Alamo." I grew up in San Antonio, so the fascination came pretty readily. In my youth, I had a pretty one-sided view of it all—the good Texans, as depicted in the John Wayne movie, against the forces of the tyrant Santa Anna. As I read more history, I saw that it was more complicated than that. I also started gaining more insights into the three noted main persons associated with the Alamo—Travis, Bowie, and Crockett. The story doesn't mean to demean at all the real men and isn't meant to be read historically, but certain facts about them allowed me to take liberties with their psyches. A lot of people who came to Texas in those days were running from trouble of one kind or another, trying to start fresh. Travis's marriage had fallen apart, Bowie had a violent past, Crockett had lost his bid for re-election to Congress, saying famously, "You can all go to hell; I'm going to Texas." So from a fictional standpoint, what great material to deal with—characters trying to remake their lives, then thrusting them into the desperate circumstances of the Alamo. I found this sort of strange comical voice of Travis's ghost to relate the tale, so I did have a lot of fun writing the story. I had some reservations—I didn't want people, I don't want people, to think I'm insulting those persons or not respecting the people who died there, on both sides...I don't have any plans right now to write about other historical figures, but I don't rule it out. One thing I'm toying around with is writing a more straightforward account of my family's early days in Texas, fictionalized but sticking closer to the truth.

LC: "My mind tends to get impatient so that I get ready to move on to the next thing. On the other hand, a few of my stories have taken over twenty years to write." Do you ever outline your stories? Would you say you're a perfectionist?

RGM: Sometimes I do a very rough outline, just a few lines, sort of like: first this happens, then that, then this...It's a lot easier to see the trajectory of a short story than the trajectory of a novel. My process is a little inconsistent. Sometimes an idea for a story comes to me and I can see the whole thing from start to finish, though maybe there are things in the middle to fill out, or maybe the story actually takes some unexpected turns as I'm writing it. Sometimes I'm writing almost half-blind, so to speak. *The Western Lonesome Society* is an example of that. As I mentioned before, I had to write for a long time before I started figuring it all out. I know John Irving has said he writes the endings of his novels first. I don't do that, but I can understand it. With my short stories, I sometimes see the ending in my mind—even though I don't actually write it. But it gives me some direction to head in, though sometimes I realize I'm not going to end up where I was first headed.

I like that there's something mysterious about writing. I think I'd get bored if I always knew what I was doing.

I think where my perfectionism comes in, is in the sound of the writing. I can hear the lines very clearly in my mind and I hear the wrong notes. Even if readers don't hear them, I hear them. Sometimes even much later, I realize I've missed something. A story gets published and I read it again and I think: Oh no! This or that word or sentence isn't right, and I wish so much right then that I could still change it. Publishing a collection is a good opportunity to catch some of that, though even then, some lines slip past me. I think, because I've been mostly a short story writer, I'm more attuned to that than I might have been if I'd always been a novelist. One wrong word or sentence in a short story can break the magical spell you're trying to create. That's kind of how I think of stories, of the effect I want—that the stories cast a sort of spell.

LC: In a long ago interview you alluded to a book you'd been working on (on and off) for a couple of decades. You said of that work-in-progress: "I've started thinking of the chapters as all being short stories in themselves. That makes each chapter sort of manageable and also gives each chapter a good crisp movement." Am I correct in thinking you were referring to *Western Lonesome*? Did this method ultimately prove effective, and would you recommend it to other aspiring novelists?

RGM: *Western Lonesome* indeed! The short story approach really helped me with this one. I see each chapter as being fun to read in itself, especially since there are a lot of characters who get their hour upon the stage. I came up with titling the chapters along the way and that somehow helped me too, gave each chapter a sort of self-contained mission, though at the same time, they were all part of the larger whole. As a guy who took fifteen years to write a novel, I should probably be careful about giving any advice to aspiring novelists! One thing that worked for me, though, and I'll share it in case it might work for someone else. My first drafts are very sketchy. I create some scaffolding and start flushing it out. So don't be afraid to just get something raw down on the page. Get something down and then you've got something to work with.

LC: You also alluded to another completed novel that you hadn't yet sold, one that was in the hands of an agent. Is this along the same lines as *Lonesome*?

RGM: Oh my, agents! My agent on my newest novel, started just a couple of years ago, suddenly informed me she was leaving the agency and moving to New Zealand. Heck of an excuse; if you want to get out of something, just tell people you're moving to New Zealand. My first agent, years ago, got evicted and started driving a cab. So I may be the kiss of death to agents. Maybe that's where "After Zombies" came from! But that novel is very different—still a mix of the comedic and the poignant, but a more straightforward novel. Again, a short one. I think I'm only capable of writing short novels. I also had two other novels, which had both been represented by agencies and came close to being published at major New York houses— one passed through several editorial readings with everyone on board to publish it and then the Senior Editor turned it down. The following week, I was working in a warehouse. Depressing. Those two novels also date back a long time, but just recently I reworked both and turned one into a very long short story, and one into a novella. I think they actually work better this way. We'll see if anyone wants to publish them. That might be some of the perfectionist in me that we talked about—I have a hard time giving up on something until I get it right, even if it takes many years. I think now if they don't get published I'm okay with it because I did with those books what I think I needed to do. Of course, I'd be really pleased if someone did want to publish them. I should mention that those are very different— they read sort of like suspense tales.

LC: You mentioned earlier your latest short story, "After Zombies," published in the current issue of *Lowestoft Chronicle*. The publication of your debut novel last month suggested you had moved on to lengthier fiction. Why this sudden move to flash fiction? And do you intend to write more flash fiction in the future?

RGM: I guess I'd say it's more a matter of working on things simultaneously. Flash fiction gives me a great break from the longer works. It can be a long stretch between publishing novels, and I need some more frequent positive reinforcement. Finishing a flash fiction gives me a sense of accomplishment and also gives me a chance of a publication without having to wait years. I'll be honest, nothing quite boosts my morale like an acceptance, and then there's the subsequent high of the actual publication. Sometimes, less makes more; some of my flash fictions are rewrites of longer stories that never quite worked. I certainly wouldn't want to work only in flash fiction, but I enjoy them as part of my overall writer's repertoire. I think maybe it's a little like writing a poem. Sometimes I write a poem, but I never really plan to write a poem, I just write a poem one day. The same thing with flash fiction—an idea comes to me and I write it. It's usually pretty spontaneous. The flash fictions give one a chance to experiment, to try out different voices and styles and ideas.

AFTER ZOMBIES

Robert Garner McBrearty

When I answered my phone this morning, my agent, Burt, screamed in my ear, "What comes after zombies? What comes after zombies?"

"I don't know," I said, "I don't know."

For weeks, we have been racking our minds on how to catch the next literary wave. We're sick of being poor, of barely hacking it. The only thing sadder than a failed writer is a failed agent.

My wife called out from the kitchen where she was burning up the oatmeal, "Is it Burt? Is it Burt? Has he sold something?"

"No, he hasn't sold anything. But we're close."

"We're always close!" She went back to burning the oatmeal.

"What comes after zombies?" I shouted at her.

"Killer squirrels!" she shouted. "A man walks into his backyard and he's surrounded by killer squirrels."

"Killer squirrels!" I screamed at Burt.

He paused. "Pitch it to me."

"Okay, okay, look. Everything appears normal. It's a Sunday morning. He goes out on his deck with his paper and a cup of coffee. Nice summer morning. His wife is inside burning up the oatmeal. The kids are at the parole officer's. He watches the squirrels in the trees. Cute. Wow, what jumpers! Look at them go, one branch to another…But something is wrong. Something is out of whack."

"What is it?"

"The squirrels are devouring something big. Something really big…"

"Like what?"

"Like a...like a deer. They've dragged a deer up into the trees and they're devouring it."

He breathed heavily. "How many squirrels are there?"

"Well, it started as a few, but now its hundreds, thousands. They're leaping over the fence. Now they finish the deer and start for the man."

"No. No, it's been done. Hitchcock. The Birds. Same old stuff, but with squirrels."

"Burt doesn't like the killer squirrels!" I called to my wife.

"Tell Burt to shove it!" She came to the doorway, waving a big wooden spoon. "Tell him to sell something or shove it!"

"What's she saying?" Burt said. "What's she saying?"

"She says to try a little harder."

"I'm trying! You've got to give me something. You've got to feed me, baby, you've got to feed me."

"Killer babies!"

"Pitch it."

"Little Oscar's in his crib. Mama reaches in, lifts little Oscar, warm and fuzzy music now, opens her dress to breastfeed... Kid goes for her jugular, blood everywhere, daddy comes in, screams, too late for him too."

Burt hesitated and then said, "No, no. It's just a redo of Jaws."

"Jaws...A sad story about a man who can't chew anymore."

"He's lost his teeth?"

"No...no...He's...wracked with a moral dilemma. He's a scientist. He's produced a kind of technology, sort of like an X-ray that reveals that the air is full of little human beings flying through the air, microscopic human beings, but with the machine he can see them clearly and whenever he opens his mouth the little men and women fly into his mouth, screaming, so if he chews, he will be eating the little human beings."

Burt made a sniffling sound. He might have been crying.

"Yuck," he moaned. "Serious yuck."

My wife stood in the doorway holding a big wooden spoon. "What's he saying now?"

"He says we need a new angle."

She waved her spoon and went away again.

"Burt?" I said. "Burt? Do you think I should just go back to writing poetry?"

"You're killing me, baby, you're killing me." Then I heard it. The sound that always sends chills through me. He was beating the phone against his head. Tap, tap, tap, beat, beat, knock.

"Alien vampire squirrels!" my wife shouted from the kitchen.

"Alien vampire squirrels…" I said to Burt.

The knocking paused. He took a breath. "Go on."

My wife stood in the doorway. Her spoon was covered in oatmeal. "Well?"

I smiled at her. "He loves it!"

MICHELANGELO DOESN'T CUT IT

Tina Koenig

My husband Michael is the Goldilocks of travel. A window seat is too claustrophobic. Coach does not have enough legroom. First class is too expensive.

There are two ways to get Michael on an airplane. Book him on a flight that is less than three hours, or tell him there is an obscure Jewish heritage site that he must see.

A six-pointed lens filters Michael's worldview and my vacations. He can find a Jewish landmark in the most goyish of places. What looks to an African rhinoceros like a muddy watering hole is actually a sacred mikvah once used by the lost tribe of Kanye West. The Great Migration? Why, that is the Jewish Exodus from Egypt, of course.

Did you know that one of the oldest temples in the United States is located in Savannah, Georgia? It is right down the road from Tara. I was surprised as anyone to learn that Buenos Aires, Argentina, has the only kosher McDonald's outside of Israel. Michael could find a mezuzah in Machu Picchu. Finding interesting Jewish places to go is as much fun for Michael as finding the hidden afikomen on Passover.

I confess, sometimes these Jewish Heritage schleps try my patience. However, they never fail to turn up something interesting—usually a member of Chabad.

Chabad is to Judaism what Starbucks is to coffee. Its Hasidic practitioners serve up a jolt of Orthodox Judaism from every corner of the world. They really should publish a travel guide.

Alas, this story is not about Chabad. It is not about Jewish Heritage schleps. This story is about Italy.

My family is of Italian ancestry. I visited Italy once when I was in elementary school. I was long overdue for another pass through the country's Roman ruins and humid art galleries.

Rather than going it solo, I booked a tour that would shuttle Michael and me through Rome, Florence, Venice, and Milan. A tour guaranteed fast entry to the Vatican, Colosseum, sites in Florence, St. Mark's Basilica, and the Doge's Palace in Venice. The hope of taking a touristy gondola ride through the smelly canals of Venice, with a hot looking tenor, had me kvelling with anticipation.

An essential part of vacation preparation is information gathering. One of my favorite sources is a little known volume published by the CIA titled *The World Factbook*. Besides snooping on unsuspecting Americans, the CIA keeps facts on foreigners and their interests. The agency compiles intelligence into a book that, rather surprisingly, is available for purchase. Among the facts collected are data on Catholics. According to *The World Factbook*, the countries with the largest Catholic population are Brazil, Mexico, the Philippines, the United States, and Italy. The country where the membership of the church is the largest percentage of the population is Vatican City, at a whopping 100%. I made a note to include this data in the briefing book I was writing for my husband. It was important that he understand there would not be any Jewish heritage breadcrumbs scattered around Vatican City.

The CIA's statistics came as a shock to Michael. Overwhelming numbers of Catholics and their heritage sites might dishearten a normal pathological Jewish trekker. Furthermore, a sensible fanatic might find the number of churches a good indicator that Italy was not a favorite vacation spot for the chosen people. A sensible compulsive might have some respect for the CIA's fact-checking abilities. Dammit!

As we were packing for our trip, I made certain expectations known. I was not participating in the usual Jewish history rummager. There would be no schlepping around. I am a petite woman. I shave my legs. I am not a Mount Sinai Sherpa.

"We are visiting a Catholic country. Do not expect to find Jews in Italy," I said in a professorial tone. "There aren't any. Not a trace. There are Romans—dead and alive. We are there to pay homage to Romans and to art."

Michael is a bit of a stereotype with coarse dark hair, a slight frame of average height, and neurotic leanings that made Seinfeld millions. And, unfortunately, like most American high school kids, he had read Shakespeare.

"That is BS." he said as he suffocated 12 pairs of underwear into a Ziploc baggie. "There were Jews in Italy. Shakespeare wrote about them in *The Merchant of Venice*."

This sudden citation of Shakespeare made me nervous. I hit back. "You can't believe everything Shakespeare wrote."

Zip. He vacuum-packed a bag of socks.

"I know there were Jewish people in Venice." He stuffed hand sanitizer into another baggie. "I read online that there is a Jewish Quarter in Venice."

"The Jews never get a fair shake," I announced. "It's always a quarter. Why is it never a dollar?"

He stopped packing for a minute to process the joke. "You stole that joke from Jackie Mason."

I had a sinking feeling about Venice and my date with the hot Italian gondola operator. I fretted that the single day we had in Venice would be spent looking for mezuzahs on the doorways of crumbling buildings.

Our first Italian tour was, indeed, the Vatican Museum in Rome. Michael busied himself sneaking unauthorized pictures of the Sistine Chapel, St. Peter's, and, later, every single Bernini sculpture in the city of Rome. Finally, I thought, this obsession with all things Jewish is licked. Michael had shifted his focus to Bernini. With a name like that, he had to be an Italian.

I was relieved when we boarded the bus that would take

us to Florence. At least on the bus we were isolated from the constant admonishment, "No photos! No photos!" It chased us everywhere.

I could not say if it is true for the whole of Italy, but in Florence, size matters.

The main art attraction is Michelangelo's sculpture of David, the Biblical figure who slew Goliath.

Known affectionately by the Italian public as "The David" (because he's the only one who matters) the young king has a special museum devoted to him in central Florence. Because our tour guide served espresso, I didn't mind the 7:00 a.m. admission time. It was early, well before other tourists arrived to wake up the museum guards and concession stand operators.

To view The David, visitors enter the Accademia Gallery through a side exhibition hall where Michelangelo's Unfinished Slaves struggle to escape the bondage of white Carrera marble. As I admired the master's work, Michael strolled toward David.

Scholars argue that the sculpture of David is Michelangelo's greatest work; perhaps one of the greatest works of art in all of time, due to its scale. Never before had a form been sculpted out of a single piece of marble that could stand on its own, without a support. Scholars believe that Michelangelo purposely engineered the sculpture so it would reflect David's strength as told in the Bible story. Masterfully carved, the viewer meets David doing the Full Monty, with no fig leaf to shield his bat and balls.

Michael and I circled the statue several times as our guide described the history and drama surrounding its commission. When we reached the front, Michael stood quietly, a quizzical look on his face. He leaned over to me and whispered, "Something is wrong."

I panicked. "Did you see someone suspicious? An unattended backpack?" I tugged on the sleeve of his shirt. "Let's get out of here."

He shook me loose. "Don't be ridiculous. Nobody dislikes the Italians. The French, the British, sure. Nobody is going to blow up The David."

"Then what's the problem?" I asked.

"There is a flaw with the sculpture," he said.

I flipped open my *Eyewitness Guide* book to the section on Michelangelo. "The tour book said there were some stress cracks and that it had to be repaired."

"It's not that. Look closely at his penis," he whispered.

"I'd rather not. There are people around."

"Don't be a prude." He pointed shamelessly at David's privates.

I tried to swat away his arm, but he had already reached into his backpack and whipped out a camera. The mechanical buzz of the zoom lens extended as his backpack slipped to the floor.

Click. He snapped a full-frontal shot. Click. He hustled to get a side view. Click. Click. Click. I grabbed the backpack and followed.

"King David was Jewish. He would have been circumcised," Michael said. There was a look of disgust on his face. "This is just wrong. Does it say in the guide book that Michelangelo was an anti-Semite?"

By now, the other tourists had started to stare at us. "You're not allowed to take pictures here," I said nervously, hoping that he would put away the camera.

"I don't give a shit," he said. "This is huge."

"I can't argue with that. It's a big dick. Twelve inches at least. He could have been a porn star for sure."

"That's not what I'm talking about. This is a major conspiracy."

When it comes to slights against the Jewish people, Michael never thinks anything is a mistake. There is always a conspiracy.

"You didn't answer me. Do you think he's circumcised?" he

asked again.

"I don't know. I've never seen an adult, uncircumcised male…in person."

I eyed Michael with curiosity. "Have you?"

"You studied art history, right?" he asked rhetorically. "Then you have to consider the question from an academic point of view. Look at it."

I inched closer to the sculpture. "It's hard to tell. Michelangelo was Italian and Catholic, what did he know about circumcised males? His Italian models likely came with the usual factory installed parts."

"The model *should* have been Jewish," Michael said. "This version of David looks uncircumcised." He twisted the camera's viewer and held it way above his own head as he continued to gather evidence of David's ding-a-ling.

"Go ask one of the docents if Michelangelo was Jewish?" he insisted. "I'm too busy."

"I don't need to ask. Michelangelo painted the Sistine Chapel on his back for fifteen years. No Jewish person would do that. They would hire someone else to do it. They hired the non-Jew, Michelangelo."

"Then ask them if this David is circumcised."

My Italian grandparents spoke a form of country Italian that they did not pass down to me. "I have a feeling that the word 'circumcised' is not in my Italian phrase book."

"It sounds like a Latin word," Michael said. "It's probably similar in Italian. Just ask in English."

I scanned the tourists circling David, hoping our guide was among them. No dice. She was probably in the gift shop where we, too, should have been. A small, dark-haired man in an official-looking docent's jacket stood talking with one of the museum guards. I approached him.

"Pardon me, may I ask a question?"

"No problem *bella*," the docent replied.

The English translation of *bella* is beautiful. The American workplace would be infinitely more civilized if all males were required to call female customers and co-workers *bella*.

I pointed to the sculpture. "Is David circumcised?" I asked.

"Circus size? Yes, it is very large," the docent said. "It is like a giant. But, no, no, no…he is not the giant. The David…he slay the giant."

"No, you don't understand." I motioned to the groin area and swept my hand in a horizontal motion to suggest chopping. "Circumcised. His genitals. Cut." I made a scissors gesture with my fingers. "Snip. Snip. Snip."

The guide grimaced. "Gentle. I no talk about gentle. No, no, no, no." He wagged a finger in my face. "You no understand. It is a big, fierce giant. No gentle giant."

I nodded my head in agreement and moved on. Why should this trip be different from all our other trips? How had my Italian Heritage Tour suddenly turned into a Jewish Heritage Schlep?

I had an art history professor in college who loved tackling questions about obscure details in paintings. When he did not know an answer he would say, "That's a great question. I wonder if someone has written a thesis on that."

As my eyes panned the walkway surrounding David, I noticed dozens of art students with sketchbooks. Perhaps one of the students cemented to the floor had written a thesis on this conundrum of the bits and pieces. I pondered a thesis title: "*The Phallic Fallacy: Representations, Considerations, and Interpretations in Michelangelo's Art.*"

I found Michael in the gift shop, shuffling through books on David, looking for close-up photographs of his *phallus maximus*. He was on a quest to uncover why the greatest artist of all time would sculpt a figure who was Jewishly incorrect.

Did Michelangelo purposely overdo David? Was he unfamiliar with the Jewish ritual of trimming the cigar?

I wondered how many other tourists had stood before the statue and pondered why the Popsicle was still in its wrapper. Of greater concern was why the CIA's *World Factbook* had no mention of a possible sect with ties to circumcision deniers. We were certain of one thing: this mission required an anatomical correction.

The subject of David's dangling participle overshadowed the rest of the entire trip. Even our gondola singer's name was David. We left Italy with no more carnal knowledge than when we arrived. It was not until we returned home that we learned the answer.

As with all things Jewish, there is an explanation—and an explanation of the explanation. Michelangelo's representation of King David is both right and wrong. The uncircumcised penis is inconsistent with modern Judaic law, but is correct according to the style of Renaissance art. According to scholars, in the time of David, only the tip of the foreskin was removed. It was not until much later that the piggy came out of the blanket. The sculpture is perfectly accurate to the time of the Biblical David.

Yet, one puzzling question remains. Everywhere else in the world, a fig leaf covers the piccolo for modesty. In a copy of David made for Queen Victoria, his bone-a-part was cloaked. Why not in Florence? Why not in Italy? This leads me to one conclusion. The Italians are, and never have been, worried about covering up anything. But, if you are worried, consult with the spies and editors of *The World Factbook*. Maybe there is something they're not telling us?

A YEAR'S WORTH OF POSTCARDS FROM LONDON

J.E.A. Wallace

King's Cross, The 20th of March

I still get a little excited
When a train pulls out the station
And we enter a beautiful limbo
Between departure and arrival

I still look for the colorful litter
Adorning the tangled embankments
Doing its best, just like the rest
Of London to emerge

And shine beneath a springtime
Whose chilly cheerfulness
Is best observed from a train window
Between departure and arrival

Greenwich, The 21st of June

We could tie the sun to a stick
By the side of this empty road
Put our backs against the trees
To watch the green grass grow

And that dirty forgotten bottle
By the side of this empty road
I think is missing its ship
We should wait for it to show

Before we go anywhere…

Chiswick, The 22nd of September

When summer's fallen asleep in the sky
And just lies there…

These giant albino mammoths
(Very slowly) crash the party
Dragging winter behind them
Like a sunburnt dehydrated cowboy

Underneath
Leaves run around on the pavement
Like cats at an old lady millionaire's house
And (finally)
The colors in this dirty old town look right

At night
The rain quietens the car alarms
And turns windows into percussion

Music to the ears
Of all the sunburnt dehydrated cowboys

Balham, The 21st of December

Outside
Icing sugar snow is falling
On a town that needs a little sweetening

The final touch
From the grey clouds' ancient fingers

The final touch?
This home of exhaust and invisible men?
I was under the impression there was further to go…

And then I realize

Throw a snowball in this town
And you'll hit your destiny.

PUEBLO CHRISTMAS

Caroline Horwitz

Large mixed-breed dogs roam through the crowds of people. There are almost as many paw prints as shoe prints in the frozen-mud ground. Beyond us are the sand-colored buildings that have stood here for almost a millennium. Beyond them are the Sangre de Cristo Mountains.

In the last hour of sunlight at Taos Pueblo, white tourists in jeans and tennis shoes or UGG boots meander across the grounds, munching fry bread and sipping hot chocolate and coffee to keep warm. We may be in New Mexico, whose name conjures scorching desert imagery, but the temperature is below thirty degrees (a blizzard ravaged the state days ago) and will only drop once the sun disappears. That's when the action will begin.

The dogs are all collarless and mild-mannered and seem to know where they're going, making their way with a purpose from one end of the pueblo to the other. They don't bother the hordes of tourists, but are friendly if approached. A big long-haired yellow one melts onto the ground and splays on his back as I pet him and scratch his belly. I see more than one visitor toss a piece of fry bread to the dogs and wonder if their owners would mind or not. Maybe these dogs don't have individual owners but are cared for collectively.

My husband and I feel silly wearing semi-formal attire here, in this sea of denim and athletic shoes. We dressed up partly because we're going to a nice restaurant for Christmas dinner afterward and because this is the closest to a religious service we will attend this season. He's Jewish but attends Catholic mass with me on Christmas and Easter.

Things are different this year. Our home is a transitory one, a hotel room on an Air Force base in southern New Mexico where he's stationed for a few months of training. Instead of traveling to Ohio to see our families for Christmas, we opted to forgo the layovers, weather delays, and harried holiday travelers to explore more of this unfamiliar state.

I see close to fifty bonfire wood stacks and hope they'll be lit soon as I curl my toes so that I can feel them again. Arranged in Jenga-like configurations, they all vary in size, with some below my knees and the two largest, at the center of the grounds, over twenty feet tall. I think about how much more height the flames will add.

We drift in and out of the ground-level rooms throughout the pueblo. All are dark and cold, but some have space heaters or kiva fireplaces. The residents display their homemade wares for sale on textile-covered tables and stone-carved shelves. Eager shoppers peruse the turquoise necklaces, feather-shaped earrings, rawhide drums, dream catchers, Christmas tree ornaments, and non-lethal tomahawks. Everyone wants some unique souvenir to show from their trip.

I am no exception. I see an ornament dangling from a wood peg in one of the shops. It's a spherical, hollow work of pottery depicting the pueblo in warm shades of paint. I take it up to the young man at the makeshift register.

"This is my mother's shop," he says, bubble-wrapping my purchase. "She makes all of the pottery in here. This is her most popular design."

He slips her card into my brown bag. I look at it outside. The store's name is The Pueblo Runner. Underneath her name is written, in quotes, "Flower Basket."

I know this must be a good day for the Puebloan people's sales, but aside from that, do they like having us here? This is their home.

Military moves have left my own sense of home far from solidified, especially lately. Most of me revels in being one half of a rootless, wandering duo, but I marvel at what it must be like to have one's entire personal and familial history, spanning hundreds of years, contained in one fixed dwelling—even if it is overrun by outsiders at times.

One by one, the firewood stacks begin to light up. The hundreds of people migrate to and huddle around the first flames, then spread into smaller groups as more are ignited. We manage to find first-row space near a medium-sized fire. In the center of the stack, as in all the others, is a small, dark green bouquet of herbs. Sage maybe, but I'm unsure. I've never grown anything. Its scent, sweet and clean, is warm in my nostrils as it burns and fills the air.

The flame grows fast. I feel it too much on my face and not enough on my feet. My brightened cheeks feel like roasting marshmallows. I'm also concerned about the proximity of the baby in the stroller beside me to the bonfire. Her mother stands behind, talking to a friend or sister. I see the orange flames reflected in the baby's eyes. It's entranced her, like a magic spell.

The two biggest wood stacks are lit from the top, requiring ladders. It takes a while for the fire to crawl to the bottoms, but once it does they are colossal, filling the sky, orange against black, miniaturizing us all. Clouds of smoke swell into gray towers. The winds pick up and move the flames laterally, chasing the warmth-seekers back a few steps.

A few minutes after five, the church bells start to peal. A blast of gunfire cuts through. People gasp and turn their attention to the bright San Geronimo Chapel where a line of celebrants has appeared. Two men at the front carry torches. The focal point is the almost life-size statue of the Virgin Mary, dressed in white, carried beneath a white canopy. It reminds me of the chuppah at our wedding, with its four posts and dipping fabric in the center. Others in the procession carry drums that they pound in unhurried unison. It's too dark to see their faces. They move as one.

Though my husband and I fancy ourselves above all the dogma, couples like us are called interfaith. This ritual could be dubbed the same, this blend of ancient Native American spirituality and traditional Hispanic Catholicism.

Low chanting radiates from the marchers as they process in slow motion, lifting the statue high above. The guns fire every minute or so, with the number of tourists who jump and inhale decreasing with each boom. They punctuate the constant sound of the drum thumps, church bells, and chanting. Drums, bells, chanting…fires crackling…drums, bells, chanting…gunshot. I'm normally jumpy at sudden noises but somehow calm each time the blanks sound.

When the procession is over and the leaders disappear into the chapel again, half the crowd leaves. The other half dwindles at the same pace as the fires. Few speak. What scarce words are spoken come out in hushed tones. We stay as long as we can stand the cold, and then it's time to leave. We're guests here, after all.

The next day, Christmas morning, my husband wraps his arms around me and buries his nose in my hair. He tells me with satisfaction that it still bears the fragrance of the herb burned in the fires.

CONTRIBUTORS

Nicholas Litchfield is the founding editor of *Lowestoft Chronicle* and author of the novel *Swampjack Virus*. He has worked in many cities around the world and has been, among other things, a journalist for a weekly tabloid newspaper, a college librarian, and a researcher for the BBC. He now lives in Western New York with his wife and two children.

Ryan Napier was born in Plant City, Florida. He has degrees from Stetson University and Yale Divinity School. His work has been published most recently in *Bartleby Snopes*, the *Bangalore Review*, and the *Lowestoft Chronicle*. He lives in Massachusetts.

Eileen Cunniffe has been writing for nearly 35 years—but the first 25 were without the benefit of a byline, as a medical writer, corporate communications manager and executive speechwriter. Her work has appeared in journals such as *Lowestoft Chronicle*, *Referential Magazine*, *Hippocampus Magazine*, *Superstition Review*, *Emrys Journal*, and *Stone Voices*. www.eileencunniffe.com.

Elaine Barnard's stories have won awards and been published in such journals as *Pearl*, *Southword*, *Timber Creek Review*, *Apple Valley Review*, *Emerge Literary Journal*, *Anak Sastra*, *Lowestoft Chronicle*, and many others. She has been a finalist for *Glimmer Train* and Best of the Net and nominated for the Pushcart Prize. She received her MFA from the University of California, Irvine.

David Havird is the author of two collections, *Map Home* (2013) and *Penelope's Design* (2010), which won the 2009 Robert Phillips Poetry Chapbook Prize. He teaches English at Centenary College of Louisiana. Since 2009 he has taught a course annually in Greece. For more about the author: https://sites.google.com/site/davidhavirdpoet/home.

Nancy Ford Dugan lives and works in New York City and previously resided in Michigan, Ohio, and Washington, DC. Nominated for a Pushcart Prize in 2012 and 2013, her short stories have appeared in over twenty-five publications, including *Blue Lake Review*, *Cimarron Review*, *Crack the Spine*, *Euphony*, *Lowestoft Chronicle*, *Passages North*, *The Minnesota Review*, *Epiphany*, *The MacGuffin*, *Superstition Review*, and *Tin House's Open Bar*.

Roland Barnes published poetry when he was young. Early in a career in psychiatric social work, he placed an article in an extinct English journal *Community Medicine*, which re-established his interest in writing, becoming a regular contributor to health, housing, and social services magazines. More recently, he has published in *The Oldie* and *Best of Britain* magazines and is currently working on two full-length manuscripts: *In Place of Cotton*, a childhood in Oldham, and *The English House*, about living in north Portugal. After living in London with his family for most of his life, they have recently moved to Swansea, South Wales, around the corner from Dylan Thomas's birthplace.

Namrata Poddar holds a Ph.D. in French Studies from the University of Pennsylvania. She was recently Andrew W. Mellon Postdoctoral Faculty in the Humanities' program on Transnational Cultures at the University of California, Los Angeles. Her criticism and creative work have appeared in *International Journal of Francophone Studies*, *Research in African*

Literatures, Dalhousie French Studies, The Bangalore Review, The Missing Slate, The Margins, Coldnoon: Travel Poetics, and elsewhere. She is currently an MFA Candidate in Fiction at Bennington Writing Seminars and English department Faculty at UCLA.

Gina Ferrara lives in New Orleans. She has published two collections of poetry: *Ethereal Avalanche* (Trembling Pillow Press, 2009) and *Amber Porch Light* (CW Books, 2013). Her poems have appeared in *Callaloo, The Briar Cliff Review, Lowestoft Chronicle*, and *Poetry Ireland Review*, among others.

Robert Mangeot lives in Nashville, Tennessee, with his wife and cats. His short fiction appears in various journals and anthologies, including *Alfred Hitchcock Mystery Magazine, Lowestoft Chronicle, Mystery Writers of America Presents Ice Cold: Tales of Intrigue from the Cold War*, and *The Oddville Press*. His work has won contests sponsored by the Chattanooga Writers' Guild, On The Premises, and Rocky Mountain Fiction Writers. When not writing, he can be found counting things or wandering the snack food aisles of America and France.

Christina Selby lives in Santa Fe, NM, with her husband and two young sons, where she co-founded an environmental non-profit organization and is a freelance writer currently working on a fiction novel. You can find her writing online and in print at *Green Money Journal, Journal for Sustainability Education, Sustainable Santa Fe Guide, Mother Earth Living Blog, Lowestoft Chronicle*, among other publications.

Ashley Mace Havird's book of poems, *The Garden of the Fugitives* (Texas Review Press, 2014), won the 2013 X. J. Kennedy Prize. Her chapbook, *Dirt Eaters* (2009), won the South Carolina Poetry Initiative Series Prize; and a second chapbook, *Sleeping with Animals* (2013), was published by Yellow Flag Press of Lafayette, LA. Her poems and short stories have appeared in many journals including *Lowestoft Chronicle*, *Shenandoah*, *Southern Poetry Review*, *The Southern Review*, and *The Virginia Quarterly Review*, as well as in anthologies such as *The Southern Poetry Anthology, IV: Louisiana* (Texas Review Press, 2011) and *Hard Lines: Rough South Poetry* (University of South Carolina Press, forthcoming). In 2002 she was awarded a Louisiana Division of the Arts Fellowship in Literature. She lives in Shreveport, Louisiana, with her husband, the poet David Havird.

Bill Cole is a school psychologist, public school advocate, and adjunct professor of developmental psychology at Fairleigh Dickinson University in New Jersey. His work has previously appeared in *Eclectica*, *California Quarterly*, and *The Great American Literary Magazine*. His fiction has also been in *Highlights for Children* magazine, for which he received their Pewter Plate Award as Author of the Month.

Justine Dymond is an associate professor of English at Springfield College, where she teaches writing and literature. Her stories and poetry have been published in numerous journals, including *The Massachusetts Review, Pleiades, Meat for Tea: The Valley Review, Lowestoft Chronicle*, and *The Briar Cliff Review*. Her short story "Cherubs" was selected for an O. Henry Prize and also appeared on the list of distinguished stories in *The Best American Short Stories 2006*. She co-edited the collection *Motherhood Memoirs: Mothers Creating/Writing Lives* (Demeter Press, 2013). She lives in western Massachusetts with her family.

Doug Bolling's poems have appeared in *Connecticut River Review, Slant, Xanadu, Water~Stone Review, Redactions, Kestrel,*

The Hamilton Stone Review, *The Wallace Stevens Journal*, *Georgetown Review*, and *Lowestoft Chronicle*, among others. He has received several Pushcart nominations and a Best of the Net nomination, and currently resides in the Chicago area while working on a collection. He is a retired English Professor.

William Quincy Belle is just a guy. Nobody famous; nobody rich; just some guy who likes to periodically add his two cents worth with the hope, accounting for inflation, that $0.02 is not over-evaluating his contribution. He claims that at the heart of the writing process is some sort of (psychotic) urge to put it down on paper and likes to recite the following which so far he hasn't been able to attribute to anyone: "A writer is an egomaniac with low self-esteem." You will find Mr. Belle's unbridled stream of consciousness at http://wqebelle.blogspot.ca or https://twitter.com/wqbelle

Michael C. Keith is the author of more than 20 books on electronic media. In addition, he is the author of an acclaimed memoir, *The Next Better Place* (screenplay co-written with Cetywa Powell); a young adult novel, *Life is Falling Sideways*; and eleven story collections—*Of Night and Light, Everything is Epic, Sad Boy, And Through the Trembling Air, Hoag's Object, The Collector of Tears, If Things Were Made To Last Forever, Caricatures, The Near Enough, Bits, Specks, Crumbs, Flecks*, and *Slow Transit*. He has been nominated five times for a Pushcart Prize and was a finalist for the National Indie Excellence Award for short fiction anthology and a finalist for the 2013 International Book Award in the "Fiction Visionary" category. www.michaelckeith.com

Frank Mundo is the author of *The Brubury Tales*. He lives in Rancho Cucamonga, California, with his wife, Nancy.

Jim Plath is an author of fiction and poetry. His work has most recently appeared in *Amarillo Bay*, *3Elements Review*, *San Pedro River Review*, *The Monarch Review*, *Lowestoft Chronicle*, and *War, Literature & the Arts*. He is enrolled in the Writer's Workshop at The University of Nebraska at Omaha.

Olga Wojtas is a journalist and writer in Edinburgh, where she attended the school which inspired Muriel Spark's "The Prime of Miss Jean Brodie." She has had a number of short stories published in literary magazines and anthologies in the UK and US, and has just won a Scottish Book Trust New Writers Award.

Nancy Scott Hanway is a graduate of the Iowa Writers' Workshop. She was recently named a finalist for the 2015 McKnight Artist Fellowship for Writers in Creative Prose. Her work has appeared in *The Florida Review*, *North Dakota Quarterly*, *Willow Review*, *Washington Square*, *Southern Indiana Review*, *Lowestoft Chronicle*, and in many other journals. She teaches Latin American literature and culture at Gustavus Adolphus College in Minnesota, where she lives with her husband and son. Please visit nancyscotthanway.com.

Colin Dodds is the author of *Another Broken Wizard*, *WINDFALL* and *The Last Bad Job*, which Norman Mailer touted as showing "something that very few writers have; a species of inner talent that owes very little to other people." His writing has appeared in more than two hundred publications and been nominated for the Pushcart Prize. Poet and songwriter David Berman (*Silver Jews*, *Actual Air*) said of Dodds' work: "These are very good poems. For moments I could even feel the old feelings when I read them." Colin's book-length poem *That Happy Captive* was a finalist in the 2015 Trio House Press Louise Bogan Award, as well as the 42 Miles Press Poetry Award. And his screenplay, *Refreshment*, was named a semifinalist in the 2010 American Zoetrope Contest. Colin lives in Brooklyn, New York, with his wife Samantha. See more of his work at thecolindodds.com.

Liz Dolan's poetry manuscript, *A Secret of Long Life*, nominated for The Robert McGovern Publication Prize (Ashville University) and The Pushcart Prize, has been published by Cave Moon Press. Her first poetry collection, *They Abide*, was published by March Street Press. An eight-time Pushcart nominee and winner of Best of the Web, she was a finalist for Best of the Net 2014. She won The Nassau Review Writer Award for creative non-fiction in 2011 and the same prize for fiction in 2015. She has received fellowships from the Delaware Division of the Arts, The Atlantic Center for the Arts and Martha's Vineyard. Liz serves on the poetry board of *Philadelphia Stories*. She is most grateful for her ten grandchildren who pepper her life and who live on the next block.

A longtime tutor, **Scott Solomon** recently launched HowtoPasstheGED.com to help adult learners gear up for the newly designed, now completely computerized GED. His fiction has appeared in the *North American Review, Antioch Review, Chicago Quarterly Review, The Minnesota Review, Chiron Review, New Letters, Other Voices, Redivider, Storyacious, Corium Magazine, Karamu, Helix Magazine, Zouch Magazine*, and *Lowestoft Chronicle*.

Robert Garner McBrearty's stories have been anthologized in the *Pushcart Prize* collection and widely published in literary journals that include the *North American Review, The Missouri Review, New England Review*, and *Narrative*. His flash fictions have appeared in *Eclectica, Posit, Big Muddy, Opium Magazine, Lowestoft Chronicle*, and *Flashfiction.net*. He is the author of three short collections, and his first novel, *The Western Lonesome Society*, was recently published by Conundrum Press. His writing awards include the Sherwood Anderson Foundation Fiction Award and fellowships to the MacDowell Colony and the Fine Arts Work Center in Provincetown, MA. His stories have been performed by professional actors at Stories on Stage in Denver and at the Dallas Museum of Art.

Tina Koenig lives and writes in South Florida. Raised as a Catholic, Ms. Koenig converted to Judaism in the 1980s. This story is one of many included in her upcoming memoir, *Confessions of a Jewish Shiksa: 36 Stories That Changed My Life*. Read more of her work at www.tinakoenig.com.

J.E.A. Wallace is a poet whose work has been published in the U.S. and the U.K., including *The Minetta Review*, *The Write Place At The Write Time*, and *Lowestoft Chronicle*. He used to be a Londoner but now lives in a tiny studio apartment in New York with his wife and the occasional mouse.

Caroline Horwitz has an MFA in creative nonfiction from Chatham University. Her work has appeared in *Animal*, *Lowestoft Chronicle*, *The Summerset Review*, and *Nevada Magazine*, among others. She lives in Las Vegas with her husband and son.

COPYRIGHT NOTES

ACKNOWLEDGEMENTS

With special thanks to Amie McLaughlin for her priceless feedback and for all the proofreading she has done over the last five years. Special thanks also to Tara for her help and advice with the magazine and her outstanding graphic design work, and to the exceptionally talented and awfully nice Robert Garner McBrearty. The magazine wouldn't exist if it weren't for the marvelous contributors we've been fortunate to publish. Much gratitude to everyone who has contributed to the magazine.

Bon Voyage!

Other titles in the acclaimed anthology series!

Lowestoft Chronicle 2011 Anthology
Edited by NICHOLAS LITCHFIELD

"This is a fine anthology that I found both provocative and enjoyable. Highest praise: it made me want to write short stories again."
—LUKE RHINEHART, author of the cult classic *The Dice Man*

"Michael Connor's 'Stevie and Louie' is a fun read about a young, single tourist in Austin…'The Shooting Party' by Jack Frey is a story of a chance encounter in an exotic location that is both plausible and mysterious. It makes good use of dialogue and an inventive plot." —*New York Journal of Books*

"All things considered, it might just be a very good thing if the Lowestoft Chronicle were to achieve their goal of world domination." —*Library Journal*

Far-flung and Foreign
Edited by NICHOLAS LITCHFIELD

"Hot off the press [is] this terrific anthology culled from Lowestoft Chronicle. The writing here is fresh, surprising, and alive. Not to be missed is the bittersweet interview with the author Augustine Funnell. (Please write more!) The book looks and feels great."
—NICHOLAS ROMBES, author of *A Cultural Dictionary of Punk*

"Nicely laid out…eclectic…humorous pieces with an emphasis on travel, hence many of the works take one to far-away and exotic places. I immensely enjoyed 'The Adventures of Root Beer Float Man' by Michael Frissore. For poetry, try Wayne Lee's 'Ordinary Deckhand.'" —*Newpages.com*

"I've enjoyed reading the *Chronicle*. 'I Like Your Deer's Moustache, and other Lithuanian Tales' …[is] a distinctly Baltic twist on mistaken identity. One of our most popular pieces." —*My Audio Universe*
(Rijn Collin's story aired on the independent radio station KVMR)

To order, visit www.lowestoftchronicle.com

Intrepid Travelers

Edited by NICHOLAS LITCHFIELD

"Without a single stinker or filler piece in the bunch. I was extremely impressed with the variety and quality of the writing. *Intrepid Travelers* is a solid collection of funny and fine travel-themed stories, poetry, essays and interviews that easily fits in a back pocket or carry-on bag."—*Examiner.com*

"Many short stories and poems here offer deeper meanings and address heavier topics. 'Something Like Culture Shock' by Dennis Vanvick…[has] good character development and a compelling story. 'Political Awakening, 1970' by Denise Thompson-Slaughter…it was refreshing to read a piece with this much depth. 'Pájaro Diablo' by Michael C. Keith…by the end, the reader is riveted to see what will happen next. Also features an interview with Randal S. Brandt…[which] has enough information and material to make for an entertaining read. Overall, this is full of great talent and exceptionally written pieces." —*The Review Review*

"Refreshing and well-written, *Intrepid Travelers* takes the reader to a wide variety of literary destinations, and makes even a confirmed hermit like me want to get up and go somewhere. Highly recommended."
—JAMES REASONER, *Rough Edges*

"Prepare for an adrenalin surge as a thief tries to escape from armed Mafia agents in Hector S. Koburn's fatalistic 'Bloody Driving Gloves,' Steve Gronert Ellerhoff's brilliantly quirky short story, 'Apophallation,' [and] Michael C. Keith's unexpectedly moving 'Pájaro Diablo.' *Intrepid Travelers* is a coruscating cornucopia of humour, drama and big, beautiful adventures. Highly original and entertaining." —*Lancashire Evening Post*

"It's unique and the quality of the writing is amazingly high."
—LUKE RHINEHART, internationally bestselling author of *The Dice Man*

Somewhere, Sometime...

Edited by NICHOLAS LITCHFIELD

"The latest collection of prose and poetry from the *Lowestoft Chronicle* is a genuine pleasure. Nicholas Litchfield has put together something very special, something to celebrate, enjoy, savor."
—JAY PARINI, bestselling author of *The Last Station* and *Why Poetry Matters*

"What a lovely book. Well designed, thoughtfully laid out, and with a grand assortment of content."
—MATTHEW P. MAYO, Spur Award-winning author of *Tucker's Reckoning*

Other Places

Edited by Nicholas Litchfield

"In the age of tweets and sound bites, it's heartening to read *Other Places*, a publication celebrating the power and beauty of a story well told."
—Sheldon Russell, author of the Hook Runyon Mystery series

"*Other Places*, a mouth-watering feast of short stories, poems, narrative non-fiction, and in-depth interviews, is the latest anthology from the much-admired *Lowestoft Chronicle*, an eclectic and innovative online journal. Packed into the pages are stories to entice, enthral, and entertain. Litchfield also serves up a tasty blend of pleasing and deftly prepared poems. And if you still aren't sated by this literary banquet, tuck into Litchfield's incisive and enlightening interviews with three critically acclaimed, multitalented writers." —*Lancashire Evening Post*

"I really loved the latest anthology from Lowestoft, *Other Places*. It's a brilliant, savory, sharp, amusing and varied taste of my favorite magazine, *Lowestoft Chronicle*. I'm delighted that a place exists for this kind of travel writing—if that's a term for it. And it's not a good one. This is just great writing about place, ranging from the spirit of place to the human spirit. Go anywhere with Lowestoft. And enjoy the trip."
—Jay Parini, internationally bestselling author of *The Passages of H.M.*

"*Other Places* is the usual delightful mix of stories, poems, author interviews, and non-fiction gleaned from the pages of the *Lowestoft Chronicle*, the only literary magazine I read on a regular basis. Always entertaining and insightful, *Other Places* is well worth your time, whether you're a veteran traveler or a hermit like me!"
—James Reasoner, *Rough Edges*

"Armchair travelers, rejoice! Editor Nicholas Litchfield has released *Lowestoft Chronicle*'s anthology for summer 2015, *Other Places*. Filled with fiction, nonfiction and poetry about travel and destinations, the book brings the far corners of the world to the reader's armchair. The stories and poems vary in tone from dead serious to delightful whimsy, offering something for every taste. Humor, adventure and mystery share the pages with intriguing result."— Examiner.com

"Sick of fly-by journalism and travel dilettantes? The antidote is *Lowestoft Chronicle*'s most recent anthology, *Other Places*—a collection of essays, stories, and poetry devoted to the in-depth experience of culture. Whether humorous, touching, or revelatory, these expertly curated pieces throw you in contact with the real."
—Scott Dominic Carpenter, author of *Theory of Remainders*

To order, visit www.lowestoftchronicle.com